You Can't Ride Two Horses With One Ass

Kurt Bartolich

Copyright © 2015 Kurt Bartolich

All rights reserved.

ISBN-10: 1519263457
ISBN-13: 978-1519263452

DEDICATION

To my mom, Joni.

CONTENTS

	Acknowledgments	i
1	Introduction: What *NOT* to Think About Brand	1
2	*You* Don't Own the Brand	4
3	You Don't Need a Mission	20
4	Stop Thinking Like a Business	38
5	Specializing Might Not Be Enough	52
6	More is Less	59
7	Stay in Your Lane	68
8	You're Only As Good As Your Words	82
9	Campaigns Are Not a Strategy	96
10	Are You Riding Two Horses With One Ass?	109
	About the Author	114
	Endnotes	117

ACKNOWLEDGMENTS

This book is the culmination of a lifetime of blessings bestowed upon me by countless people. Even if it was just briefly or for a lifetime, at work or play, professional or personal, platonic or romantic, our intersection was premeditated. I'm absolutely sure of it.

I'd like to start by thanking the people who put their time, talents, and (more than) two-cents worth directly into this book, including Kris Kendall, Christine Moore, and Barbara McNichol—three gifted editors who built upon each others' input and direction, preserved my voice, and proved that a word is really worth a thousand pictures; Katie Zogleman, my attorney, for watching out for my backside; Stacy Furey, for being an extra set of eyes—twice; Teresa Carey, Pat Maday, Robin Rottinghaus, Ethan Beute, Shawn Honea, and Cory Scheer—all leading professionals in their respective industries that gave me invaluable feedback on my manuscript; and Julie Kraft, Karen Cottengim, Teresa Carey, and Pat Maday, who let me tap into their expertise and granted me permission to recite their wisdom.

I'm grateful for Jim Steinlage, the late Dick Cray, and the partners at Choice Solutions, who took a chance on me after I first hung out my shingle.

Special thanks to Edie Howard, my *friend of truth*, who always seems to know the right time to smack me upside the head with pearls of wisdom.

Thank you Kelsey, Stacy W., and Stacy L. for your unwavering love, unconditional support, and for putting up with my puns.

1 INTRODUCTION: WHAT *NOT* TO THINK ABOUT BRAND

The year was 1994, and I was attending an annual broadcast marketing and promotion managers conference in New Orleans. At the time, I was the promotion manager for KAKE-TV, the ABC affiliate in Wichita, Kansas. One morning, I was reviewing the roster of concurrent seminars I could attend but nothing caught my eye. So, I randomly chose one about "branding" by a couple of guys I'd never heard of before: Al Ries and Jack Trout. In full disclosure, I selected this session because the room was closest to where I was standing. I sat in the back, figuring I could slip out easily if I got bored. Little did I know that fate had intervened.

About the moment I was stuffing my conference-issued bag under my chair, I jolted upright as if I'd been doused in ice-cold water. Did I just hear what I thought I heard? Did this Ries guy actually say, "A successful brand narrows its focus to stand for one thing"? I couldn't believe my ears.

As Ries unfolded evidence of how this principle equates to market dominance, the hair on the back of my neck stood up. Though I had never heard it expressed that way before, *it was exactly how I was positioning the television station.* In that moment—seared in my mind forever—I realized my calling. It wasn't television; it was brand.

Some 10 pages of notes and an hour later, I found myself buying the Ries-Trout session tapes and everything else with their names on it (yes, they're also brilliant marketers). Included in my Ries-Trout stash was *The 22 Immutable Laws of Marketing*. While many great books have been written on this subject, in my opinion, this book is the brand "bible." It guided me until I found my own voice, which I share in this book.

While *The 22 Immutable Laws of Marketing* once catalyzed my becoming a brand practitioner, *You Can't Ride Two Horses With One Ass* is the culmination of more than 25 years of study, practice, and maturity. Why the name *You Can't Ride Two Horses With One Ass?*

I first heard this expression used by an account manager with a client and I immediately recognized how it embodies everything I believe about branding. Intuitively I knew it was the perfect title for a book about brand conservancy. Indeed, it evokes the whole spirit of this book. At its essence, *You Can't Ride Two Horses With One Ass* focuses on the repercussions of your personal ethos on your company's brand. Conscious or unconscious, what goes on between your ears has more influence on your brand's success than what happens in the marketplace.

This is not a how-to-*build*-a-brand type of book; rather, it's a how-to-*protect*-your-brand book. Consequently, by following the ideals, tenets, and precepts expressed within these pages, you will also create a blueprint for birthing, repositioning, or growing your brand.

I'd be remiss if I didn't state that no client, company, or branding professional cited here has approved, sponsored, or endorsed the statements, opinions, or philosophies in this book. They are my opinions based on the facts available to me. Accordingly, certain statements about why a brand action or decision was made and the effects of certain actions may not be accurate according to those directly involved at the time. When applicable, though, I do introduce third-party expertise, perspective, and evidence for supporting the premises and ideas you'll read here.

Open your mind to this brand doctrine filled with pitfalls to avoid—an assurance that, by applying the wisdom between the front and back covers, you can protect *your* most valuable asset—your brand.

– Kurt Bartolich

2 *YOU* DON'T OWN THE BRAND

Only history will determine if President Barack Obama's second term—and perhaps his overall legacy—will be defined by his effort to guarantee health insurance for all Americans. Calling his universal health plan controversial is like saying the sky is blue. I'll leave the politics to the pundits and focus on a different side of this conflict between government and "we the people"—the name.

The White House prefers Americans call this health plan the Affordable Care Act. In a surprising compromise, it would even let you refer to it as the ACA. Yet a 2013 CNBC poll revealed that 30% of people surveyed didn't know what the ACA was, but only 12% were unfamiliar with the term Obamacare.[1] So why, despite the insistence of those in power to do otherwise, do most people call it Obamacare? Much to the chagrin of the President's inner circle, even Obama uses the slang name.

In another naming example, the H1N1 pandemic got everyone's attention in 2009. The World Health Organization (WHO) implored the media to stop using the slang term, "swine flu," citing it as a "factual error." The U.S. Department of Agriculture made a stink about it, too, alleging that hog farmers, their workers, and their families suffered as a result of the street name. Yet, the name swine flu stuck.

When I did a Google search the terms Affordable Care Act and H1N1 returned 64 million and 7.1 million results, respectively, compared to Obamacare (15.5 million) and swine flu (5 million), respectively. That means there were over 400 times more references online for the proper names than the nicknames. So, why did these nicknames stick in the public's minds? Contrary to its own petition, the WHO knew why, as a spokesperson for the organization said: ". . . of course we're a scientific organization. A (H1N1) is a scientific name. That's it. But the scientific name is not very user friendly. I think it would help all of us if we could find a name that's easier to say that's more popular."[2]

This is akin to what's called Tommy John surgery, the accepted name for ulnar collateral ligament (UCL) reconstruction first performed on Los Angeles Dodgers' pitcher Tommy John and many athletes' elbows since then.

In contrast, surgery for the ACL—anterior cruciate ligament—is performed on knees of professional athletes, weekend warriors, and anyone else who sustains a severe injury to that ligament. While ACL procedures date back to Egyptian times, Tommy John surgery has only been around since 1974. So, why do people use the ACL term so much more than UCL? Well, one reason is ACL got there first so UCL needed a name that wouldn't sound like it. Second, Tommy John was one of the best pitchers in baseball at the time. By comparison, the first ACL procedure was likely performed on a no name—that is, not anyone noteworthy to connect it to. Too bad Tutankhamun didn't blow out his knee. King Tut Surgery might have caught on.

In another example, around 2006 the American Red Cross minimized the usage of the Heimlich Maneuver technique and the name, replacing both with "back slaps" and "abdominal thrusts." It stems from a difference in opinion between Dr. Henry Heimlich, who invented the method that bears his name, and the Red Cross, which cited "lack of evidence" that his technique worked better than back slaps.[3] However, this might be an instance when using a popular brand name could have life-saving implications. I for one don't want to be choking in a restaurant when someone shouts, "Does anyone know abdominal thrusts?"

Who *Really* Owns the Brand?

Would you think a company called Choice Solutions has a distinctive or memorable name? I certainly didn't when I started consulting with this IT Solutions Company. But I'm not a proponent of conjecture, so I had this name tested in a pilot brand study my firm conducted for them. Good thing I held my tongue. To *its* consumers, the name Choice Solutions meant everything because it imbues the spirit of impartiality. In the study, the idea of being "unbiased" was one of the highest rated motivators for choosing an IT partner. Choice Solutions it is!

These examples and a myriad others I could reference illustrate two important points. First, if a name is strategic and also unique, simple, and memorable, it's got a much better chance of being permanently stored in the hard drive between the customers' ears. Second, it's not about names; it's about who's the boss of your brand—and that ain't the people inside your company or organization. It's your *consumers*. After all, it's customers who started saying Tar-*zhay* for Target and Chevy for Chevrolet.

One business that truly understands consumers are at the helm of the brand is Overland Park, Kansas-based Freedom Bank. In 2006, Kurt Knutson, then a 25-year industry executive, started Freedom Bank to address consumers' growing impatience with long lines and lack of privacy[4].

Unlike most banks that still have an institutional layout, Knutson brilliantly engineered a physical space that more resembles the lobby of a W Hotel than a traditional bank. It has a concierge desk at the entrance, private banking rooms in lieu of teller windows, and a guest plaza that doubles as an event space for client use. There's a bar that provides coffee by day and drinks at night for catered events. It even has a video game area to keep kids entertained. In this way, Freedom Bank was engineered to address its customers needs more than its own. It should be little surprise then that Freedom Bank grew from $21.8 million in assets to $144.6 million by the end of 2014[5].

Freedom Bank embodies what many other companies and organizations fail to recognize or accept: *Consumers* are the proprietors of brands, while companies are the caretakers.

Proof of Consumer Ownership

A few years ago, a surveillance technology company realized it might benefit from gathering intelligence on its brand. So in addition to the people in law enforcement—the users of surveillance technology—we administered the research to employees to check for any misalignment. The results showed 50% of the staff members perceived their employer as a solutions company but less than 10% of its consumers saw it that way. Conversely, 45% of its consumers recognized it as a technology company compared with only 12% of its employees.

In other client examples, an IT company was perceived as a "reseller" by its consumers while it saw itself as a "consulting" firm, and leaders of a Kansas community believed "history" defined its image but visitors insisted it was the unparalleled beauty of its tall grass prairies, rolling hills and wide open spaces.

Why does such disparity matter? Because "a confused customer buys nothing," according to Annette Franz Gleneicki, VP of Customer Experience at Touchpoint Dashboard, a firm that maps customer journeys to help companies improve the customer experience. She explained, "They (confused buyers) won't return—at least not without a lot of effort from you and, perhaps, from their friends—and they won't recommend you, either. On top of that, they develop this dissatisfaction that leaves a general bad taste in their mouths about your brand."[6]

Sometimes an image has to find its beholder—like the now defunct Honda Element. The Japanese automaker launched its "dorm room on wheels" in 2002 for Gen "Y" buyers. American Honda's vice president at the time said, "The Element resonates with a younger audience." Except it never did. Price and young people not liking it when older adults tell them what is good for them were cited as reasons Honda's boxy SUV was out of its element. The median age buyer ended up being 42, and by the end of the decade it was 52. Not coincidentally, sales were off target as well. Only 14,000 Elements were sold in 2009—way off from its peak of 84,000 in 2003. The end of the road for the Element came two years later.[7]

Accepting that it's the people buying from you who own the brand can create a seismic shift in the way you do business. It also runs counter to the famous Henry Ford quote arguing against this: "If I had asked people what they wanted, they would have said a faster horse."

If you're creating something never seen before or something that will start a category, revolutionize the world, change mankind, spawn cottage industries and countless technological innovations, create millions of jobs and constitute billions of dollars in annual sales, then by all means, go for it! If, however, your brand is like most that are birthed into existing categories, it's imperative you crawl inside your consumers' heads to understand their unmet needs and gaps in competitors' offerings.

Think about it this way: Would you ever let a doctor perform surgery on you without at least taking an X-ray?

Playing Russian Roulette With Your Brand

With so much at stake, why do so many companies continue to operate by the seat of their pants? For example, a company that builds box making and assembly equipment had expressed interest in having my firm calibrate its brand position. After a six-month courtship, the owner suddenly changed his mind. His reason? "I have a year's backlog on machines and more coming, so I guess I don't have a branding problem; I have a fulfillment problem," he wrote to me in an email. His response brought up several questions in my mind. Did the concern he had before about the clarity of his brand magically fix itself? Was the backlog a byproduct of something his company was doing or a competitor wasn't? Was he winning business on price or was it a value proposition his customers recognized (and he might not) that could allow him to charge even more? He was guessing and that's *not* a strategy. It's the equivalent of playing Russian roulette with your brand. Knowing what drives business growth from the consumer perspective *is* a strategy and can help you avoid the rollercoaster revenue ride that besieges so many businesses.

Case in point. Samsung spent three times more than Apple on consumer research, and it made the South Korean electronics manufacturer a formidable challenger to Apple in the smartphone category.[8] Samsung isn't gobbling up market share because it makes better phones; it's doing so because it uses *real evidence* to make smart decisions.

Had my surveillance technology client not listened to its customers and proceeded with a plan to bring a consumer version of its product to market, it would have killed its credibility with law enforcement officers—its primary customers—and likely its brand.

The Perils of DIY Research

Maybe worse than having no consumer insights is conducting do-it-yourself (DIY) research. During a meeting I had with partners of a law firm, one of the lawyers tried to make the case that they should do the research instead of us. He argued that gathering testimony and analyzing evidence is the essence of what lawyers do. Here is the culmination of that conversation:

> I asked, "Would you ever recommend that someone represent himself in court?"
>
> "No," the lawyer replied.
>
> "Why not?" I redirected.
>
> "He can't be objective," he said.

Clearly, the irony was lost on him. With DIY research, impartiality goes out the window. Yet objectivity is what would dramatically increase the law firm's chances for success—*and* yours.

DIY (or as I prefer to call it "country club" and "parking lot" research because it takes place subjectively and unscientifically) is usually unreliable because the methodology, sample, and analysis are flawed. For example: A home improvement store collected receipt surveys from customers and noticed a pattern of complaints about not being able to find help at times. It translated this as meaning it didn't have enough employees. But our research showed them the issue was actually *lack of access to knowledgeable employees*. Had the client relied on its own interpretation, it likely would have thrown more bodies at the problem. Not only would it have been costly it wouldn't have addressed the real issue. Instead, it developed a new training model and re-engineered the store layout so customers could more easily access knowledgeable employees.

Attempting to do your own research is akin to diagnosing your own illness or doing your own financial planning. Not only is the chance for making a mistake greater, you also can't emotionally detach. That's because a DIY research sample is often comprised of friends, family, golfing buddies, employees, and sometimes random strangers. The first problem: These people are unlikely to be your target customers. Then when you put them on the spot, they're more inclined to tailor their responses to please you. It's human nature. As University of Virginia psychologist Bella DePaulo first noted in a 1997 *Psychology Today* article (and is still widely used for reference today), "Lies make it easier for people to get along."[9]

DePaulo co-conducted a diary study of 147 people between the ages of 18 and 71 and found that one in every four of the participants' lies were told solely for the benefit of another person. The article also noted, " 'Fake positive' lies—those in which people pretend to like someone or something more than they actually do (e.g., *Your muffins are the best ever!*)—are 10 to 20 times more common than 'false negative' lies in which people pretend to like someone or something less *(e.g., That two-faced rat will never get my vote)*."

Pamela Meyer, author of Liespotting, said in a 2011 Ted Talk: "If you got lied to, you agreed to get lied to. Lying is a cooperative act." She added that particularly in business, "We are against lying but covertly for it."[10] Essentially, we hear what we want to hear, *not* what we need to hear.

With DIY research, you'll get an earful of horse manure.

Surveys vs. Studies

When it comes to brand development, companies don't need opinions. They need real insights obtained objectively and scientifically.

To that point, a distinction needs to be made between surveys and studies. A survey is akin to polling: It's typically one dimensional—focused mostly on addressing the "what"—and only useful for soliciting general opinions. As such, the outcomes aren't terribly reliable. Look no further than the final political polls leading into the 2016 Iowa caucus—the first preliminary for electing our president. According to the Iowa Poll, real estate mogul Donald Trump held a five-point lead over Texas Senator Ted Cruz in the race for the Republican nomination.[11] But the actual results from the Iowa caucus were flipped with Cruz winning by four percent over Trump.

In contrast, a study can provide perspective in three dimensions—the "what," "why" *and* "how"—and provide real insights into attitudes that influence behaviors. With the right sample, a study will deliver a high degree of confidence that the findings are accurate and the outcomes can translate to a larger market.

The truth is DIY research conducted by companies and organizations—and many agencies for that matter—are really just polls passed off as surveys. Based on the results of the Iowa caucus, would you trust a survey for your brand?

Purity of Data Not Everything

Even if you're already on the objective third-party research bandwagon, you have to be judicious with the results and understand how to interpret them for your brand. Far too often, I've seen recommendations made to companies based on the purity of data. For example, a 2012 study of a technology client's customers and prospects revealed that IT security was their top motivator out of a dozen tested for choosing a consulting partner. On face value, the data would suggest the client brand itself as delivering the best IT security. But this would have overlooked the fact that a competitor already owned the security position. Since copying others is not a viable brand strategy, we had to dig deeper into the research to find a different position. The needle in the haystack turned out to be an idea around "virtualization" and it's contributed to a 60% spike in company revenue in three years.

Leave It To The Experts

When it comes to brand territory, the advice is about to get personal. Yes, I'm speaking specifically to owners, CEOs, and heads of companies or organizations. Far too often, I encounter executives who believe they're also research, brand, and marketing experts. This manifests itself in many ways, including their insistence on reviewing all advertising, calling on their inner circle to make marketing decisions by committee, and even rewriting copy. But having general knowledge of something does *not* make one an expert. If that were true, a family doctor would perform heart surgery. There's a reason they're called *general* practitioners!

Granted, when it comes to most company decisions, it's usually the leader's head on the chopping block. But when you pick apart every sentence of a marketing brochure, you're not leading—you're controlling. I suggest you focus more on strategic decisions around the brand—in particular, protecting it from bad ones like Ben Gay Gum, Bic Underwear, and Heinz Mustard. Brands that get stretched too far like those aren't just funny anecdotes. They can inflict real damage on the credibility of the core brand in customers and employees heads, and set businesses back millions of dollars in wasted R&D, marketing, and advertising. Worse of all, it can open the door for competitors.

Olive Garden is proving to be a shining example of how brand preservation *is* a strategy CEOs should focus on. Under new leadership, it's eliminated operational and menu excesses and gone back to the basics: Pasta, meat, cheese, and sauce. As a direct result, overall sales increased 12% in the first quarter of 2015 and stock for its parent company, Darden Restaurants, surged 4% to hit an all-time high.[12]

If leaders don't have confidence in their marketing people, then they should upgrade the talent. If they think the marketing department exists to serve the head of the company, then they themselves are the problem. The marketing department—and *every* department—has one purpose: To curate the brand. So, if you're guilty of nit-picking every sentence, put down the pen and become what the organization needs most from the corner office: A brand cop that makes sure everything the company does works *for* the brand and not *against* it.

Of course, not all leaders and their employees will be on the same page all the time. As a leader, when you think a message is off point but your marketing people don't, don't fight it out subjectively. Even though you've earned the right to have the final say, pulling rank will only drive a wedge between you and them. Taken further, it could potentially damage your reputation among other internal stakeholders. When employees feel it's "us against them (leadership)," you jeopardize your vision being realized and company objectives being met.

Therefore, make your case for change based on facts, not fiction. Third-party evidence gathered from customers and prospects is the ultimate mediator. I tell my clients they can push back on me until the cows come home but because I represent their consumers, they're essentially arguing with their customers! Fighting with your consumers is one war you'll never win.

Level the Playing Field

Taking a non-partisan position requires having evidence gathered by third party and sharing the insights with your employees. That way, you can create a level playing field by mandating all challenges be rooted in what your consumers need, not what employees want. Stripping away the subjectivity will both galvanize your employees toward common goals and intensify their engagement. These are essential to driving bottom-line performance in your organization.

Poet and activist John Alejandro King neatly summed up the value of understanding your consumers' attitudes this way: "If you want to read the fortune, you have to break the cookie." That means to truly unleash your brand you have to accept that consumers are the proprietors of it and company stakeholders are the caretakers of it. You also have to "break the cookie of consumer attitudes" to understand what drives customer behavior.

If you can win mind share, you will control market share.

3 YOU DON'T NEED A MISSION

A signature method of mine for teaching people brand is the slogan test. Here's how it works. I show participants a few slogans such as "Apply Happy," "So Good," and "The Power To Do More." Then I ask them to name the brand associated with these slogans. Most people whiff on all of them (if you were a professional baseball player striking out that much, you'd be looking for a new career). I then ask them to identify the brands associated with "lip balm," "fried chicken," and "computers sold direct to home." Most of them nail all three: ChapStick, KFC, and Dell. For the record, the first group of slogans belongs to these same brands in order.

This illustrates that a brand is not a slogan. A brand is a *position* people link only to you, and it's based on an objective idea or concept. Slogans are typically subjective and often fail to convey a company's position. How many companies, products, or services could fit "Apply

Happy" (job website, greeting card line, etc.), "So Good" (a beverage, dog food, etc.), and "The Power To Do More" (a lawnmower, investment firm, etc.)?

Therein lies the problem. If you can put your slogan on any other brand and consumers would be none the wiser, then it won't work for *you*. The same applies to company missions. Most are watered-down horse crap that reeks of compromise and out-of-touch leadership. Here are two examples:

> Brand X will produce superior financial returns for its shareowners by providing high value-added logistics, transportation and related business services through focused operating companies. Customer requirements will be met in the highest quality manner appropriate to each market segment served. Brand X will strive to develop mutually rewarding relationships with its employees, partners and suppliers. Safety will be the first consideration in all operations. Corporate activities will be conducted to the highest ethical and professional standards.

> Brand Y's brand mission is to be our customers' favorite place and way to eat and drink. Our worldwide operations are aligned around a global strategy called the Plan to Win, which centers on an

exceptional customer experience—People, Products, Place, Price and Promotion. We are committed to continuously improving our operations and enhancing our customers' experience.

Those boardroom-endorsed masterpieces came from leading shipping and fast food companies, but they could adorn the walls of virtually any business in America—and that's also a problem. Does anyone inside companies with missions as watered down as beer at a frat party even notice them? More important, do they guide, govern, and motivate employees?

Mission Statements Don't Spark Engagement

Gallup research has shown that leaders leveraging their mission to maximize employee engagement can be a strong predictor of business success.[13] They also found that typical mission statements are ineffective at spurring that engagement. As another Gallup article pointed out: "Every individual has a unique sense of purpose and individuals find different meanings in similar situations. Thus, the proverbial mission statement does not necessarily help employees find a sense of purpose in their work. There is nothing wrong with mission statements but they are often too vague and too broad to allow every employee to connect with them."[14]

I disagree with that last point. There's *everything* wrong with missions that are too vague and too broad to create connection. That's why every company and organization should have a *brand mission* instead of a traditional one. What's the difference? While traditional missions typically focus on company performance, a brand mission distills organizational purpose. An exemplary example is Ritz-Carlton's brand mission: "We are ladies and gentlemen serving ladies and gentlemen." It is the soul of the luxury hotel brand and beating heart behind its reputation as the gold standard in service.

Even The Apple Store uses Ritz's elite service as a benchmark, and has adopted many of its engagement techniques such as anticipating customers' unexpressed needs (transferring their data to new devices and teaching them how to use products), resetting their internal perceived wait time clocks (allowing them to play with other products and other employees instigating short, personal interactions), and owning the relationship (escorting customers around instead of pointing and checking back on them after they've been handed off to someone else). [15]

The Ritz's accolades include it being the only service brand to win more than one Malcolm Baldrige National Quality Award. With standards such as every employee being empowered to do what it takes to resolve a customer issue, and preparing rooms for returning guests based on their preferences from previous stays, it's easy to see why.

In contrast, those missions cited for the shipping and fast food companies do nothing to inform employees about how to engage customers. Virgin Founder, Richard Branson, understands how important it is to make your mission intentional: "You need to explain your company's purpose and outline expectations for internal and external clients alike. Make it unique to your company, make it memorable, keep it real and, just for fun, imagine it on the bottom of a coat of arms."[16]

Think of a brand mission as what sheet music is to an orchestra: It ensures everyone is playing in the same key.

Closing the Gap Between Purpose and Brand

Far too often, there's a chasm between the company's purpose and the brand customers expect. But a brand mission can help you bridge that gap because it embodies your "why" (purpose), "how" (differentiation), "who" (target consumers), and "what" (customer expectations). In short, a brand mission is your organization's True North—defining who you are and who you aren't—and beacon for guiding what you should do and what you shouldn't do.

Every organization needs a brand mission to ensure that the promise your brand makes and the payoff your consumers expect are one and the same. Essentially, what you say you do is what you *always* do. Teresa Carey, founder and president of Performance Pointe, which develops leaders and provides organizational strategy to Fortune 500 companies in Pre-Rapid Growth stage, defined the brand mission this way: "It's how they (employees) show up, each and every moment when conducting business." Like the on-duty janitor who, when President Kennedy asked him during one of his visits to NASA, "What do you do?" he replied, "Well, sir, I'm helping to put a man on the moon."

Creating Organizational Guardrails

Google is guided by "You can make money without doing evil." Dyson is governed by "Solve the obvious products others ignore." Whether you call these values or purpose or "why" statements, they function like a brand mission because they provide a cultural compass for focus and compliance.

You can make money without doing evil is an organizational guardrail that bans pop up ads and any ads on results pages, and requires a "Sponsored Link" to identify advertising. All of these imperatives are designed to protect the integrity of its search results, including a self-imposed embargo on selling the white space on its home page—even though it's potentially worth billions of dollars in additional revenue. *You can make money without doing evil* cascades into other company decisions like preserving its focus on being one thing—search—and the fidelity of the YouTube brand after acquiring it in 2006. By adhering to its brand mission, success has followed. In 2013, Google was five times more profitable than Bing and Yahoo! combined.[17]

Solve the obvious problems others ignore is the cultural ambit that prevents Dyson, a British manufacturer of vacuum cleaners, hand dryers, bladeless fans, and heaters, from bringing ordinary products to market. Without that brand mission, its products would probably look, perform, and cost about the same as a Hoover—a fine vacuum but no Dyson. Instead, Dyson's relentless drive to reinvent the wheel—er, ball—is why its products can command three to four times more than most other brands.

Brand Mission Coherence

Any company or organization could learn a lot about coherence from the Amish people who look to The *Ordnung,* a set of unwritten rules and regulations, to guide everyday Amish life. This includes their plain dress code and bans on electricity, automobiles, television, divorce, and running for political office. Much like a brand mission should shape culture, the purpose of the *Ordnung* is to uphold community.

Some Amish sects practice Rumspringa, a Pennsylvania Dutch term for "running around." Rumspringa is a period of time in which adolescents are granted what's essentially a "get out of jail free card" to rebel. Depending on the Amish district, Rumspringa can include driving, television, cell phones, smoking, drinking, all-night parties, and sex. It's essentially a culture test with only two possible outcomes: Defect or return to the Amish way of life. In some cases, less than 10% fly the coup.[18] Even the best companies fall well short of *that* retention rate.

Brand Mission Establishes Priorities

Having a clear brand mission is instrumental in establishing priorities. This is mission critical because not everything is of equal importance to your consumers. Here's an example.

For decades, KMIZ-TV in Columbia, Missouri, was the skinny kid that got sand kicked in its face. Meanwhile, KOMU, the University of Missouri-owned NBC affiliate and the university's incubator, represented the muscle in the market. KOMU had parlayed the school's decades-old reputation as the best journalism program in the country into a winning local news position. It was reminiscent of the way the University of Kansas

Medical Center has leveraged "teaching hospital" to conquer the Kansas City hospital market.

But things changed for KMIZ in 2008. A year prior, it had hired Frank N. Magid Associates, a global research and strategy firm in entertainment and media. At the time, I was working for Magid as a brand consultant and assigned to KMIZ along with news consultant Pat Maday. We led KMIZ leadership through a brand-mission-defining process that resulted in this gem: "We always keep TABS on Mid-Missourians." TABS stood for Tracking, Alerting, Breaking and Safekeeping, which were among the most significant viewing priorities for news consumers in the market. But at the time, those news coverage priorities weren't being adequately or consistently met by any local brand.

TABS, as it affectionately became known inside KMIZ, epitomized standards of vigilance for all stakeholders and set expectations of "no nonsense news" for viewers. "Is that TABS?" became the newsroom mantra and filter for all content decisions. If it wasn't TABS, it wouldn't be in a newscast because it wasn't a priority for local news consumers.

"When they (KMIZ leaders) developed a brand (mission), they developed a culture," said Maday. "Suddenly, everyone knew who they were and what they were supposed to be for the audience. It didn't take long for that audience to notice and appreciate the change." Indeed, KMIZ made up nearly two decades of ground in less than two years and eventually dethroned KOMU. At the time of this publication, it remains entrenched in the spirit of TABS and number one in viewership ratings.

It's important to point out that KMIZ's rapid transformation occurred as a result of *commission* and not *omission*. All employees—not just those who produced the content that was broadcast or posted—were responsible for delivering on the brand promise. For example, the brand mission made it clear to engineers that the technology enabling them to execute TABS was their new priority, to management which capital expenditures took precedence, and to salespeople what content was off limits for client sponsorship to avoid cheapening the brand. TABS was the station's sextant for synthesizing a culture of purpose.

KMIZ's success also epitomized the real definition of branding: How you walk the walk.

Brand Mission=Promise Kept

Gallup recently surveyed 18 million consumers and found that only half of the companies they do business with deliver on what they promise. More startling, 62% of them are indifferent or actively disengaged with those companies.[19] This makes them vulnerable and more open to switching brands. Ensuring seamless and consistent delivery on your promise requires a brand mission and a strategy to bring it to life in everything you do. Mulready's Pub in Emporia, Kansas, has done this quite impressively.

Opening its doors in 2013, Mulready's has already been featured on the Discovery Channel's TV series *BarHunters*, and it's quickly gaining a reputation as a little slice of Dublin in East Central Kansas. Arguably, the driving force behind its success is its declaration, *"We Don't Slop Drinks"*. Not only does it tick all the right brand mission boxes—unique, concise, specific, and actionable—it leaves absolutely no doubt about what Mulready's stands for and against. Whether you gather around a table, sit on the patio or belly up to the bar, you won't see any plastic cups, a doorman, food other than pretzels and peanuts, and hear it referred to as a bar because it's a "pub." Glasses are sprayed with water between pours to enhance the taste and all employees are Cicerone trained—a program that "certifies and educates beer professionals in order to elevate the beer experience for consumers"—to cultivate Mulready's "Know Thy Beer" character. [20]

Suppose Mulready's had gone the typical route and created something like this: *"Our mission is to consistently provide friendly service in a comfortable atmosphere where our patrons can enjoy quality drinks."* Not only is that worth less than the paper it's printed on, it is also the price of admission.

It's like a car rental company saying: *"Our mission is to provide rental cars that will start."* Without a brand mission, your employees won't know what to expect or how to create unequivocal experiences that give consumers a consistent reason to choose your brand over all others. When unique value is absent, consumers make purchasing decisions based on default factors such as lowest price, convenience, or familiarity with an employee—none of which are controllable or sustainable.

Just like people who always change their story, brands that say one thing but do another are hard to trust. If Alcoholics Anonymous attendees were permitted to drink once a week, Harley-Davidson made a scooter, and St. Jude Children's Hospital treated adults, would they be as credible as they are now?

Remember, brands do not get days off.

Slogans Should Be "Mini" Brand Missions

Let me emphasize that a brand mission should never be confused with a slogan. While a brand mission is focused internally, a slogan is externally facing. However, a slogan should also convey your unique value and create accountability for all company stakeholders.

Papa John's "Better Ingredients, Better Pizza" slogan states a promise to consumers and therefore should serve as a standard for employees. However, it could be argued that Fritos as a topping is pushing the definition of a better ingredient. Fuzzy boundaries not only have the potential to damage public perception; they can set dangerous precedents organizationally. How can you justify to one employee that Fritos is a better ingredient but to another peanut butter isn't?

Brand Mission Don'ts

The ambiguity and business jargon often found in traditional missions attack company credibility. Trendy words like "disruptive," "synergy," "value add," "dynamic," and "sustainability"—and my all-time favorite, "core competencies" (if your goal is to be competent then you must presently be incompetent)—might seem harmless but a 2011 study by New York University referenced in the *Personality and Social Psychology Bulletin*, revealed that business jargon makes people think you're lying.[21] It goes on to say "concrete statements allow us to create mental pictures more quickly...when something is more easily pictured it seems more plausible, so it's more readily believed." By avoiding vague language and jargon in your brand mission, you can foster certitude instead of uncertainty.

It's also important to avoid superiority claims in your brand mission because they are about the company, not the consumer. They are also results, not reasons for choosing a brand. One aspiration of Pizza Hut as noted in its mission statement is "to take pride in making the perfect pizza, provide courteous and helpful service at all times and strive to have every customer say that they plan to be back." In contrast, Papa Murphy's, whose "take and bake" brand has made it the fifth largest pizza company, said on its website: "At Papa Murphy's we are fresh fanatics. We come in early to make our dough from scratch, grate our 100% whole-milk mozzarella every day, and hand slice our veggies." Recent data from Techmonic's Consumer Brand Metrics indicated that customers are most likely to return to Papa Murphy's (and In-N-Out Burger) among the 128 leading restaurant brands tracked.[22] So, let met get this straight: Pizza Hut states it wants to be "best at intent to return" but *isn't* and Papa Murphy's doesn't say it but actually *is* best at it? Actually, this shouldn't be a surprise to anyone. Hope is never a strategy but a brand mission *is* one.

Brand Mission is Ideal Brandometer

Unlike traditional missions and banal slogans, a brand mission is the ideal brandometer for measuring cultural compliance and consumer adoption.

It's easier to benchmark performance against "We Are Ladies and Gentlemen Serving Ladies and Gentlemen" than something like "Deliver a franchise success system of strong brands, exceptional services, vast consumer reach and size, scale and distribution that delivers guests, satisfies guests and reduces cost for hotels owners." With a brand mission serving as the touchstone, you could measure success factors such as alignment between employee and customer perceptions (like effectiveness in delivering on the brand promise), track employee engagement (through decreases or increases in customer loyalty), and define standards for compliance (such as the staff must always take bags to the room and rooms must be prepared based on guests' preferences from previous stays).

Brand Mission is Personnel Polestar

A brand mission should also be your organization's polestar for personnel decisions. Because a properly constituted brand mission is cloaked in objectivity, it can eliminate much of the subjectivity that goes into qualifying, acquiring, and retaining talent. As Jim Collins, author of *Built to Last* and *Good to Great*, said in a 2013 *Forbes* article: "If you think paying higher wages than your competition is the solution to hiring the best people, you would be wrong. The right employees for your organization must be driven not by money but by your organization's mission." [23]

Karen Cottengim is founder of True North Career Strategy, a firm that specializes in matching candidates to companies based on cultural fit. She explained that, in today's competitive job market, a company's brand mission could be a huge differentiator in attracting candidates. She says, "Savvy companies recognize that everyone in the company is a brand ambassador and they make sure the talent acquisition team and hiring managers are on the same page in identifying candidates who are the right fit. They understand how to demonstrate their brand mission throughout the recruitment process, communicating frequently and clearly, so candidates are not left in the dark."

Cottengim adds, "Companies that weave their brand mission into hiring and performance management processes often experience an added benefit of higher employee retention and engagement."[24]

Zappos, an online retailer known as well for its culture as its shoes, is so committed to finding the right talent to help it deliver on its relentless service promise that it will pay new hires $2,000 to *quit* after the first week of training if they decide it's not the place for them.[25] Similarly, Mulready's Pub only seeks people who are as passionate about beer as the founders are.

To retain your best talent, you have nothing better in your arsenal, including higher wages, workspace flexibility, or more time off, than a brand mission and a record of coherence to it. A 2013 international Gallup study of nearly 50,000 business units across 192 different organizations found this: "Ensuring employees have opportunities to do what they do best every day and emphasizing mission and purpose are the two strongest factors for retaining Millennials, Generation Xers and Baby Boomers."[26]

Rita Bailey, 25-year veteran at Southwest Airlines and former director of its University for People, might have said it best: "Hire for attitude. Fire for attitude."[27]

As I like to say: If you're not working *for* the brand, then you're working *against* it.

Brand Authenticity Trumps All

Google, KMIZ, Ritz-Carlton, and Mulready's are transcendent examples of what is the soul of any brand: Authenticity. While it's a term carelessly thrown around with such frequency it's at risk of becoming the new "paradigm shift," its absence will expose your brand as a fraud and potentially doom it. Millennials—people born between the early 1980s and early 2000s depending on whom you ask—is the group with the largest number of consumers today. Virtually every brand including churches covets this generation's involvement. In the U.S., 59% of people ages 18 to 29 quit going to church at some point.[28] How do churches respond to attract this group? "Cooler bands, hipper worship, edgier programming, impressive technology," said Rachel Held Evans, blogger and author of *Searching for Sunday: Loving, Leaving and Finding the Church*. However, Evans cited research from Barna Group and the Cornerstone Knowledge Network that indicated two in three millennials prefer a "classic church" to a "trendy" one, and more than three-quarters would choose a "sanctuary" over an "auditorium."

"Millennials exhibit an increasing aversion to exclusive, close-minded religious communities masquerading as hip new places in town," proclaimed Evans. "For a generation bombarded with advertising and sales pitches—and for whom the charge of 'inauthentic' is as cutting an insult as any—church rebranding efforts can actually backfire, especially when young people sense that there is a more emphasis on marketing Jesus than actually following him."[29] The lesson here for all businesses: Don't pander and don't try to be something you're not. Be yourself. No one is more uniquely qualified.

A brand mission can help you stay true and *is* the True North every organization needs to reinforce their purpose, foster employee engagement, create customer loyalty, and provide governance for *all* people, processes, and standards—*all* necessary elements to drive company performance.

4 STOP THINKING LIKE A BUSINESS

I had always found it paradoxical—and rather self-serving—that some of the big retail pharmacies sold cigarettes and provided walk-in health clinics under the same roof. So, when CVS Health announced in early 2014 it would stop selling tobacco products, I was suspicious. Its leaders' decision to kick the habit was praised by health care organizations, the medical community, and even President Obama. Company president and CEO Larry J. Merlo explained on TV why his company snuffed out tobacco this way: "Put simply, the sale of tobacco products is inconsistent with our purpose."[30]

While I commend CVS for adding tobacco education and smoking assessment programs, let's not hastily award it the Presidential Medal of Freedom. Instead, let's put it into perspective. It's estimated CVS would lose $2 billion in revenue with this move, and while that's a lot of dough, it's merely 3% of the company's total revenue.[31]

CVS Health has proclaimed on its website that "health is everything." If that's true, what about the candy, soda, and processed foods its stores still sell? Most of these products are loaded with GMOs, sugar, high fructose corn syrup, and artificial sweeteners—all known to contribute to obesity and other health problems. Why don't those run counter to CVS's purpose? While it's not public knowledge what percentage of revenue is derived from sales of those products, it does beg this question: Is CVS motivated by its bottom line or its brand?

More importantly, do *you* think like a business or like a brand?

Business Thinkers vs. Brand Thinkers

In my experiences, company leaders are inherently either business thinkers or brand thinkers—mostly the former and less often a mix of both. What are some of the key differences? Business thinkers are usually governed by spreadsheets while brand thinkers are guided by research. Business thinkers fixate on *market* share while brand thinkers focus on *mind* share. Business thinkers tend to be imitators, impatient, and tactical and brand thinkers tend to be original, patient, and strategic. But the biggest difference is this: Business thinkers typically put profits ahead of people while brand thinkers put people ahead of profits.

Nowhere is this more evident than in the airline industry. Most domestic carriers suck our wallets dry with fees for ticket changes, checked bags, snacks, and more. I classify them as business thinkers. But Southwest Airlines has no baggage or change fees and doesn't nickel-and-dime consumers. It's a brand thinker. With over 40 consecutive years of profitability, Southwest Airlines knows the perks of being a non-stop brand thinker.

That's not to say that Southwest Airlines is strictly mission over margin. The company can be as miserly as the next guy—maybe more so. Specifically, it only flies 737s to control maintenance and training costs. It only sells tickets on its website to cut out the middleman. And no baggage fees means more luggage is preloaded which reduces time spent at the gate checking bags, accelerates passenger loading, and gets planes off the ground faster—all of which keep revenue soaring.

If you didn't know these facts about Southwest, you're not alone. Unlike most of its competitors whose financial transparency borders on pan handling, Southwest's business model is virtually opaque. That means its business and brand models are so fused, they are hardly distinguishable from each other. When Southwest makes a business decision, it has a net positive impact on the brand. When it makes a brand decision, it has a net positive impact on the business.

Think of it this way: If all airlines eliminated their rewards programs, which ones do you think would experience the least amount of financial turbulence? If J.D. Power's 2015 North American Airline Satisfaction Study were any indicator, Southwest Airlines, which ranked second only behind Jet Blue for low-cost carriers,[32] would likely just keep on cruising. The narrative that accompanied the study noted: "When passengers make the decision to fly an airline based on the services or experience the airline provides rather than price or convenient routes and scheduling, satisfaction is higher and passengers are substantially more likely to return to the airline brand and to recommend it to others."

Brand Wise, Business Foolish

However, a brand thinker who makes poor business decisions is just as likely to struggle or fail as a blatant business thinker. Consider Kmart and its blue light brand that once ruled low-end retail before Wal-Mart came along and forced it into price wars.

Unlike Wal-Mart with its "just-in-time" inventory system, Kmart failed to set up modern supply chain management, which helped seal its fate and a 2002 date with bankruptcy.[33] In another example, usually brand *and* business savvy Target announced in early 2015 it was pulling out of Canada less than two years after it crossed the border. While American brands Wal-Mart[34] and Starbucks[35] continue to perform well in Canada, Target's series of business and operational blunders—bad locations, higher prices than in the U.S., empty shelves, and overzealousness in opening 124 stores in the first 10 months—led to $2 billion in losses and ultimately its retreat.[36]

I'd be remiss if I didn't point out that Wal-Mart has been successful north of the border in part because it runs its Canadian operations through its international division. As such, it treats Canada as a different place with unique cultures, needs, expectations, and competitors. Speaking from my own consulting experiences there, if I heard this once I heard it a thousand times: "Do not try to Americanize us!"

What's the lesson? Be prescient and conduct research with your potential consumers before expanding into any new market. It's the best way to discern the nuances of geography, competition, culture, values, ethnicity, gender, social economic status, politics, and other factors so you can position your brand for success in a different market.

Transactions vs. Relationships

In the 1987 film *Wall Street*, its fictitious villain Gordon Gekko infamously told shareholders, "Greed is good." In reality, greed is bad for your brand. Quoted in a 2011 *Forbes* article, Roger Martin, dean of the Rotman School of Management at the University of Toronto, said, "If you take care of customers, shareholders will be drawn along for a very nice ride."[37] Even Jack Welch, former CEO of GE and once the king of shareholder value, has done an about face. In a 2009 *Financial Times* interview, he said, "On the face of it, shareholder value is the dumbest idea in the world. Shareholder value is a result, not a strategy."[38]

It's easy to spot companies whose leaders are all about making a quick buck rather than making customers for life. They tend to have higher customer churn and employee turnover, rollercoaster revenue statistics, and incentives for employees to sell more, cut costs, and improve efficiency. Typically, a transaction-driven tone is set at the top of the organization. Here's an example.

I was once privy to a directive from a company leader with instructions to "push the brand stuff out after hours so as not to interfere with business." Do you suppose such words have ever been muttered inside relationship-driven companies like Nordstrom, Zappos, or Chick-fil-A? *Those who treat brand as a department or an activity simply don't get why they're there.* As management guru Peter Drucker said in 1973, "The only purpose of a firm is to create a customer." While I agree in principle, the modern take on it should be: "The only purpose of a firm is to create *prophets*." After all, when Drucker made that statement, companies had fewer competitors, smaller footprints, and were dependent on traditional advertising.

Today, creating consistent profits requires creating *prophets*—those who are unwavering in their commitment to your brand and carry a torch for it—but that can only happen when you are relationship driven not transaction focused.

Focus on Efficiency Can Hurt Brand Efficacy

Today, business decisions take on many forms and can manifest themselves in different and often insidious ways. One of them is an emphasis on improving efficiency through streamlined processes or automation. Typically, the payoff is a reduction in manpower and payroll. But far too often, the strategy backfires, resulting in pissed-off customers—like yours truly.

I once considered Enterprise my rental car brand of choice. However, the last few times I rented from this company, the center didn't have any cars—*even though I'd made reservations well in advance.* Isn't having cars the price of admission for any rental car company? It's like going to a bank that doesn't have any money. During one particular experience, I had to wait an hour until the rental agent found a vehicle for me. Worse yet—and counter to its *"We'll pick you up"* promise—*I* was the one who had to go to a different location and do the picking up! For my troubles, I wasn't charged for topping off the tank, which makes me wonder how much Enterprise might be giving away in comps. I also wonder how much stress employees feel when having to play the auto shell game.

When I asked why this Enterprise center had no cars, the agent blamed it on a switch to a centralized reservations system. He tried to reassure me the kinks would eventually get worked out. I couldn't verify if that was actually the issue. Still, the fact remains the center didn't have cars and didn't live up to its promise, suggesting an underlying issue with its operational/business model. Tired of feeling second in this relationship, I'm courting a new rental car brand. I wonder if Avis still tries harder?

One Cannot Be At the Expense of the Other

Whether you're a business or brand thinker, know this: One cannot be at the expense of the other. Having a business model that doesn't support the brand or a brand that is difficult to monetize, will impede growth. For example, a company that has a brand rooted in whole solutions but a sales force better incentivized to sell individual products will create internal friction and external confusion.

In another example, a former client in law enforcement surveillance technology was contemplating expanding the business into the consumer market. However, our research revealed that even under a different brand name there was a strong possibility the move would damage the credibility it had built over 25 years among law enforcement officers. One agent who responded to the study put it best: "It's hard enough trying to send undercover officers into drug buys with equipment. If people other than

LEO (law enforcement officers) can buy it, before long, bad guys will know all our tricks." In this case, it wasn't only the company that would have been at risk.

When it comes to execution, brand *is* business strategy. Case in point: Southwest Airlines' business model has enabled the company to consistently make brand decisions. Sure, it could charge bag and ticket change fees like its competitors but would it be as beloved? Leaders like Southwest may be operating a business but they make decisions like they're running a brand.

Don't Relinquish Control

What if you're forced to make a business decision that could negatively affect your brand? Kansas City is famous for barbeque and Oklahoma Joe's was a local legend that perennially topped national "best of" lists—which says something when you consider all the other local BBQ joints turning up on the same lists. Of its three Kansas City locations, Oklahoma Joe's signature site was in a gas station. That's where, in 2014, President Obama dropped $1,400 on an Air Force One take-out order[39] and a month later New Jersey Governor and 2016 presidential candidate Chris Christie dined. It's such a destination that typically there are only a few days each year when you won't see a line out the door and around the corner—Sundays and holidays when the restaurant is closed.

But in the summer of 2014, Oklahoma Joe's announced it was changing its name to Joe's Kansas City Barbeque. Talk about brand—and barbeque—blasphemy! The Oklahoma Joe's brand transcended food. It was an experience and a Kansas City institution.

Now, I spend a great deal of time helping clients create brand names and protect the fidelity of them in the minds of consumers. I'm steadfast in my belief that a brand name attached to a differentiating position *is* your competitive advantage. Therefore, I believe you should do everything within your power to maintain jurisdiction over your name—with one big exception: When you no longer have complete control of it.

For context, Oklahoma Joe's started in Stillwater, Oklahoma, in 1996. A month later, partners Joe Davidson and Jeff and Joy Stehney opened the Kansas City gas station location. In the late 1990s, Davidson sold the Oklahoma location and moved to Texas, but the Stehneys maintained control of the Kansas City market. In 2011, Davidson opened a new Oklahoma location and a year later another in Tulsa, both under the Oklahoma Joe's banner. That's around the time the Stehneys and Davidson met and amicably worked out a separation plan. Davidson would retain the name but stay out of the Kansas City market until 2021. The Stehneys would have to rebrand their locations in Kansas City. Considering all the equity they had built into the Oklahoma Joe's name, no one would have blamed the Stehneys if they'd fought to retain it. However, by relinquishing it, they took the fate of their brand out of the hands of Davidson, who plans to expand nationwide.

No one knows if Davidson's chain of Oklahoma Joe's restaurants will maintain the same standards that barbeque connoisseurs have come to expect in Kansas City. But one way or the other, his moves would impact the Stehney's brand, and they weren't about to let that happen. "While we come from the same tree, we have slightly different variations in our recipes," Jeff Stehney told *The Kansas City Star*. [40] "But it became apparent that while I own the Kansas restaurants, I don't own all the rights. The value of my brand could get diluted."

This is the kind of introspection you'd expect from a brand like Apple or Southwest Airlines, but it's a way of thinking *everyone* should embrace. A brand that remains in control of what it can and relinquishes what it can't is less likely to compromise its most valuable asset: Its image. A brand might not technically be intellectual property but you should always treat it as such.

Don't Gamble with the Brand

Sadly, for every example like Oklahoma Joe's, there are far too many others that relinquish control of their brand to someone or something else. One leader in a small Kansas community had expressed a desire to better understand who was visiting his city. He wanted us to conduct research on why people came and what their perceptions of the community were. Unfortunately, the Chamber of Commerce board didn't share his sagacity. Instead, it wanted to wait and see what impact a casino would have on the city's image after it was built.

Now, if you're a business thinker, the casino is a no brainer. If you're a brand thinker, you would wonder if a casino would tarnish the city's image. If the other community leaders were being brand wise, they would attempt to find out what perceptions the casino would have on the community before green-lighting the project. At the very least, they could determine how to position it within the city's brand. What the board doesn't get is it's rolling the dice with its brand and allowing the casino to potentially reposition the city. The legendary Jack Welch took risks at GE but he didn't gamble with the brand. "Control your destiny or somebody else will," he once said.

While true, it's rarely one brand that knocks off another. Usually, brands succumb to self-inflicted wounds. Despite owning multiple digital patents, Kodak's own myopia about the consumer shift to digital photography has been brand suicide. Blackberry's failure to recognize that people want a device for more than just business has been a bullet to its brand. And then there is MySpace. While many believe Facebook rendered the near crippling blow, lack of focus has really been its hara-kiri. Sean Percival, vice president of online marketing at MySpace from 2009-2011, said one of the social media pioneers' main failings was bloat like featuring too many celebrities, fashion, sports, and even books. "Facebook has done a really good job of not doing that . . . Lesson learned: do one thing great, not do many things good," said Percival. "Or in our case, we were doing many things kinda crappy."[41]

The lesson for any brand: Control your position or risk *being* repositioned.

It's How Your Consumers Think

Why is it so important to think like a brand? Because consumers do. It's why they buy Crest and Lipton, not P&G toothpaste and Unilever ice tea.

The truth is this: Consumers really don't care about your business. They only care about what's in it for them—i.e., your brand. Put another way, when you're focused on feeding the business, you will starve the brand. And that's a bad way to do business.

5 SPECIALIZING MIGHT NOT BE ENOUGH

In the late 1970s, comedian Steve Martin coined the phrase "Let's Get Small." It was the title of a comedy album by the iconic star of standup, screen, and stage, but he could have very well been talking about brand.

I've always believed the secret to making your business bigger regardless of the size of company or organization is to make your image smaller by specializing. But even niche things such as vinyl records, Palm Pilots, and aerobics run their course or are quickly supplanted by advancements such as digital music players, smart phones, and CrossFit. Some categories, many non-technical in nature, inspire little imagination in the eyes of consumers like banking, chiropractic services, and insurance, to name a few. For some brands, specializing simply might not be enough. Instead, you might have to "Get Even Smaller." Or, as I prefer to call it, micro-specialize.

A little context about our current place in time might be helpful to understand micro-specializing. In today's wired (and wireless) world, boundaries are no longer defined geographically. Brands appear virtually at our fingertips—sometimes tens of thousands in as little as 0.13 seconds. Then there's the physical saturation. For example, in the five-mile radius around my office, you'll find:

- 200-plus non-fast food restaurants
- More than 50 places that will fix my computer
- About 35 plumbers who will unclog my toilet

At one time, endurance running, laptops, and social media were specializations. Today, they've evolved into macro-specialties—or categories if you prefer—which have paved the way for micro-sports (Warrior Dash), micro-computers (tablets), and micro-media (Twitter).

How does a specialization morph into a macro-specialization? Typically, it spawns a host of imitators, often with indistinguishable differences, or it breeds new species. Unofficially, Facebook begot "posting" and inspired Instagram for "(photo) sharing" and Twitter for "commenting." Unless you set up residency first in consumers' heads when a specialization turns into a macro-specialization, your brand could get evicted. The demise of MySpace, a precursor to Facebook, reminds us of the importance of owning, not leasing, mental real estate.

Becoming a Micro-specialist

A micro-specialist is something or someone that hyper-focuses within a macro-specialization. For example, Dave Stockton is a professional golf coach, which is already a macro-specialization. However, his overt focus on the short game makes him a micro-specialist. Ask world number one and four-time major champion Rory McIlroy how being coached by a micro-specialist has worked for him. In another example, even within the already exclusive Navy SEALs is an elite unit known as SEAL Team 6—the micro-specialists who took out Al-Qaeda leader Osama bin Laden in 2011.

A micro-specialist is likely to inspire word-of-mouth growth among legions of like-minded consumers. For example, people who suffer from migraine headaches but don't like the hangover-like effects of some medications would benefit from The Migraine Relief Chiropractor, a micro-specialization we birthed. During our primary and secondary research for this chiropractor, we found a legion of migraine suffers seeking drug-free solutions and willing to pay an out of pocket premium for it. This example shows that, with the right micro-specialization, you can build a successful, profitable brand without a big investment.

Smaller Pool, Bigger Profits

Some of my clients have expressed concern that micro-specializing will shrink their potential customer pool. While that can be true any time you focus, the trade-off is often the ability to charge more.

In 2011, my firm was engaged by a rather rare dentist to clarify his practice's brand. He was one of only 2% of dentists performing dental implants, oral surgery, endodontics, periodontics, and prosthodontics himself. But having this multi-discipline expertise created confusion among his staff and with his patients who struggled to articulate what kind of dental practice it was. Our solution was to create a micro-specialty called "Pentadontics." This represents the integration of those five dental disciplines into one modality to restore the most complex mouths in fewer appointments. Not only has micro-specializing helped clarify his practice's image, unify the message, and provide a compelling point of distinction, it has shown signs of being a lucrative move. A former employee shared with me that the Pentadontics practice was able to command fees well into five figures for a single case. How many general dentists could command the same? Yes, a micro-specialist can create macro-profits.

Transcendent Impact

Teresa Carey was already successful at developing leaders and providing organizational strategy to Fortune 500 companies when something began to pique her interest. The founder of Performance Pointe had observed many organizations ascending into rapid growth without a rudder. That absence of strategy typically created a reactive climate and a company culture without a compass to navigate the waters ahead. Seizing the opportunity, Carey became a micro-specialist when she launched a new stage in the lifecycle of businesses. We coined it Pre-Rapid Growth.

Pre-Rapid Growth is the stage just prior to rapid growth. Carey's firm now micro-specializes in helping company leaders proactively and seamlessly maneuver through this "make or break it" period. The benefits of micro-specializing to her brand have been exponential. "Being an expert creates a stronger value proposition" said Carey. "As soon as I started focusing in on more specialized services based on clients' Pre-Rapid Growth needs, business increased."

The benefits of micro-specializing for Carey have extended beyond her bottom line. As she said, "It accelerates decision-making, creating efficiency in how I analyze and evaluate potential scenarios. I find it liberating, and I don't feel pressured into taking work that doesn't align with my brand. I can be authentic and true while maintaining my brand integrity. It's like a GPS."

Another benefit to micro-specializing is its inherent ability to clear up uncertainties and clarify expectations on the *other* side of the table. "Being a micro-specialist takes the guesswork out of the value equation and the deliverable for clients," noted Carey. "They know specifically what they're getting and the tools their leaders need to navigate that stage of growth successfully. They get it right away."

Should You Micro-specialize?

Every company, category, and marketplace is different. However, aspects to consider are the trajectory of your company's revenue, the girth of your margins, and your momentum in the marketplace. You will also want to take into consideration factors about your category, including how congested and innovative it is, and what place you occupy.

I suggest the most important analysis should be a deep dive into the attitudes of your consumers to find out if they see your brand as unique and essential to their lives. Because attitude tends to drive behavior, if you understand the attitudes of your customers, you can influence their behavior. That calls for objective research. Conducting the right kind of study can help you determine if micro-specializing is right for *your* brand.

Steve Martin also once said, "Comedy may be big business but it ain't pretty." This too could describe brand positioning. Micro-specializing might not always make you the coolest or biggest company, but in today's rapidly evolving and fragmenting world, it might be the shrewdest way to protect your brand and foster prosperity.

6 MORE IS LESS

The year was 1980. Disco was dying, the Reagan era was beginning, and an amateur hockey team from the U.S. was slaying the mighty Russians in what became known as The Miracle on Ice. It was also the last year that the poor folks east of the Rocky Mountains were denied Coors beer, at least legally. As a result of a self-imposed prohibition, Coors had achieved cult-like status. It was rumored that while in office, President Ford "smuggled" a case of it back to the White House, and Paul Newman refused to be seen drinking any other brand on screen. There was even a movie about bootlegging Coors in 1977 called *Smokey and the Bandit*.

In 1999, a new game show hosted by Regis Philbin premiered on ABC with little fanfare. A year later, *Who Wants to Be a Millionaire* was rewriting the ratings record books. With 29 million viewers on average per broadcast, it was more like *Who Wasn't Watching Millionaire?* It also spawned a host of new game shows and essentially revived unscripted TV. However, two years later, the audience had all but vanished and the show needed a lifeline of its own. By 2002, network executives finally pulled the plug.

In the early 1990s, Starbucks was brewing up a storm and became one of the fastest growing companies in the U.S. By 2006, it had nearly 12,500 worldwide locations and had turned the ordinary coffee shop into a caffeine sanctuary. However, by the middle of 2008, its stock had dropped faster than a coffee bean in a grinder—down 50% from the year before.[42] Starbucks proceeded to close 900 stores and cut thousands of jobs.[43]

Overexpose, Underperform

Far too often, companies mistake more locations, more shelf space, and scaling as growth strategy. I contend that the biggest mistake Coors, *Millionaire*, and Starbucks made was thinking mass availability equated to mass consumption. A 2009 article about the demise of *Millionaire* captured how too much of a good thing proved to be a bad thing for the brand. "The question that has always surrounded *Millionaire* is whether ABC got hooked on what competitors called the 'ratings crack' it provided and ran the phenomenon into the ground by scheduling it four times a week at its peak. Certainly the show flamed out quickly once its popularity began to fade."[44]

Midway through 1981, the same year Coors began selling beer east of the Rockies, Coors Light was still an infant, Bud Light was still in the womb, and Miller Light—credited with birthing the light beer category—was turning six. Some pundits contended that the emergence of light beer hurt Coors (9% drop in annual sales in the 1980s and 1990s.[45]) more than making it available to everyone.

If that's true, then what explains Budweiser's continued growth during that same timeframe, which peaked at 50.4 million barrels sold in 1988?[46] While Coors Banquet Beer experienced resurgence in 2013, it's still a third of what it was in the mid-80s.[47] Perhaps the answer to fixing the brand has been under its nose all along. On the Coors website, you'll find this reference about the impact that limiting distribution once had on its brand: "... this created a strong mystique to the brand. Tourists often returned to their homes in the east with trunks full of Coors beer."

Some have speculated that the recession that was starting around 2007 hurt Starbucks most. After all, how could people justify $5 for a cup of coffee when they weren't even sure if they'd be getting another paycheck? But if a tanking economy was truly to blame, how do you explain what happened with Apple, Chipotle, and Ralph Lauren? They didn't just survive; they thrived. Ralph Lauren opened 100 new stores in 2009[48]; Apple's revenue mushroomed from $24.6 billion in 2007 to $65.2 billion in

2010,[49] and Chipotle's net income ballooned from $70.56 million to just shy of $179 billion during the same stretch.[50] You might expect discount retailers like Wal-Mart or Costco to benefit from a cratering economy but not Apple, Chipotle, and Ralph Lauren—all premium brands near the top end of price point in their respective categories.

In another head-scratcher move, in 2007 Starbucks started installing drive-through windows. For the record, I was chastising the move long before the first disembodied voice pronounced, "Welcome to Starbucks . . . May I take your order?" To this day, I'm still met with opposition—many who argue that more accessibility will lead to increased brand loyalty. Do you think the guy with an $80K Mercedes in his driveway feels more loyal to the brand when his neighbor pulls up in a $30K Benz? Maybe I've sniffed a few too many coffee beans but when was Starbucks' brand ever about *convenience*? It was originally a destination not a fast food-like joint. In fact, it was a brand of *inconvenience* with a big ole' welcome mat inviting people to stay as long as they want, sip venti double shot skinny lattes while catching up with friends, conducting business, cruising the Internet, listening to Starbucks' select music, perhaps even purchasing some tunes or a pound of its signature roast. In CEO Howard Shultz's book *Onward: How Starbucks Fought for Its Life Without Losing Its Soul*, he stated Starbucks' mission and social contribution: "*To inspire and nurture the human spirit—one person, one cup and one neighborhood at a time."*[51] Tell me, how do drive-through windows feed the human spirit?

What Were They Thinking?

Is Starbucks really building more loyalty, or is it riding two horses with one ass? Any brand that tries serving two masters—inconvenience and convenience in Starbucks case—serves neither. It also makes your brand vulnerable to a one-trick pony.

Here's a similar example. In 2001, Mercedes Benz rolled out its $25,000 C230 hatchback. At the time, John Wolkonowicz, a partner in Northville, Michigan-based consulting firm the Bulin Group, told a *New York Times* reporter, "When a premium brand becomes available to the common man, it casts doubt on the legitimacy of the premium of the company's other products and diminishes their value. As soon as a brand tries to be everything to everybody, it loses focus in the mind of the consumer."[52] According to goodcarbadcar.net, which tracks auto sales data, there's evidence Mercedes indeed took a wrong turn. By the end of 2007, the C230 was a bad memory, but the perceptive damage was done. By 2009, domestic sales of the S-Class had sunk to a seven-year low and the E-Class was reeling from consecutive years of declines between 2004 and 2008.[53] Meanwhile, domestic sales of the Lexus ES grew steadily and set a company record in 2007 while its ES brother quadrupled sales from 2004 to 2005.[54]

It seems Mercedes didn't learn its lesson. In a move that likely would make Britney Spears proud, oops, Benz is doing it again by introducing the $30K B250. In contrast, its nemesis Lexus has gone on record stating it won't chase Mercedes down at that price point or even for global sales domination. One might say Toyota's upscale sibling is throwing in the towel. I say it's focusing on what matters most: Its brand!

Understand this: Lexus is typically a luxury leader in dealership experience[55] and resale values[56] according to J.D. Power and Associates. To get to the $30K level, Lexus would likely have to strip amenities such as powered seat cushion extenders, ventilated seats, memory systems, 5.1 stereo surround, intuitive parking assist, and possibly safety technology such as pre-collision warning and lane departure alert systems, to name a few. You'd be left with a Camry. While a Camry is a fine car, it's no Lexus.

Be Exclusive, Not Inclusive

A few years ago, I was introduced to Cliff and Debbie Van Till. The down-to-earth farmers from California relocated their family to the rural community of Rayville, Missouri, and opened a new farm-to-table business. Capitalizing on their uncanny ability to grow, make, and bake almost anything, the Van Till's business ended up being part winery, part restaurant, and part bakery. As a result, they didn't experience the growth they had expected so they turned to my firm to help them clarify the brand.

From the research we conducted, the Van Tills faced several important decisions that would determine the direction of their business and the fate of their brand: Should it be a restaurant, winery or bakery?

They also had another critical choice to make. Just like Wal-Mart can't be expensive, Mini Cooper can't be big, and KFC can't be healthy in consumers' minds, Van Till Family Farm Winery can't be both a retail *and* a destination brand. This was true particularly since their vision was to have people spend the day there soaking up the rural vistas, sipping their wines created from the area's unique, nutrient-rich soil, and pairing them with their artisan wood-fired pizzas. Making their wines available online and in liquor stores would, in essence, be *their* Starbucks drive-through window.

How well did sequestering their brand work? The Van Tills estimate winery revenue has increased tenfold since 2011. Because they don't offer their wine on a retail basis, the Van Tills don't have to worry about pricing relative to competitors or against themselves at the winery. It can sell a bottle of wine in the wine shop for $25, and sell they do. While some nearby competitors struggled, Van Till Family Farm Winery was growing more than just grapes.

Tone It Down to Build It Up

If your brand is suffering from overexposure, it's not too late to tone it down as Starbucks did in 2008. It closed all of its 7,000-plus U.S. stores for a day to refocus, retrain, and get back to the coffee culture it had created.[57] You might consider reducing the number of locations, products, services, or SKUs in your portfolio. Perhaps you need to be more discerning with distribution, retailers, and partnerships.

You could also learn a lot about brand restraint from the Jacob Leinenkugel Brewing Company of Chippewa Falls, Wisconsin. This shrewd, third-generation family beer maker has steadily been brewing up Shandys—beers mixed with a non-alcoholic drink—and a storm in the craft beer category with its limited release strategy. By restricting availability by seasonal windows, Leinenkugel's has created "Shandymonium." A September 2013 CNBC article referencing Nielsen data indicated that nearly 10% of craft growth year-to-date came from the Leinenkugel Shandy line, and Summer Shandy was the fastest "turning" national craft beer on the market.[58] Perhaps the answer to the Coors Banquet Beer inconsistencies is right under their own roof; Leinenkugel's parent company is MillerCoors.

In case you haven't noticed, the only place you can get airfares for Southwest Airlines is on its website, Joe's KC Barbeque is in Kansas City, and Summer Shandy is, well, in the summer. So instead of making your brand more inclusive, you might want to make it more exclusive. For the record, the top two busiest Starbucks stores are near Times Square in New

York City and the original in Pike Place Market in Seattle. Neither has a drive-through window.[59]

7 STAY IN YOUR LANE

If I had a dollar for every time I've been told I'm too rigid about brand, I'd be sitting on a beach sipping Coronas (because it's the beach beer after all). Most of the criticism levied against me comes from colleagues and peers, but sometimes it comes from clients. Most often, it's driven by their desire to "broaden our focus." But isn't that an oxymoron like "anarchy rules," "barely dressed," and "one size fits all"?

It's true that I have little tolerance for any brand that can't stay in its lane. For example, Dominos Pizza has recently expanded its menu beyond pie and is justifying it by dropping "pizza" from its name and going by just "Dominos." Jimmy Dean is "not just for breakfast anymore" and Smith and Wesson apparently believe if you can fire one of its guns, you can ride one of its bicycles. This continues happening in the face of compelling evidence that shows nine out of every ten brand extensions fail, according to Al & Laura Ries, branding experts at Ries and Ries.[60]

Crossing the Line

Even wallet-stuffing Wall Street tends to get bullish when brands take detours. For example, on the heels of announcing its new premium milk brand in early 2015, Coca-Cola got a less than warm reception from investors as its stock dropped.

The magazine *Car and Driver* is known to kick more than tires when a brand veers off course. This opinion came from a 2015 online review of a new SUV: "Like hair extensions, brand extensions make us wince. We like authenticity. But no matter how deeply ingrained a brand's identity, that identity still belongs to a company, not a church, and a company's first priority is not adhering to a belief system, it's making money. Given that, the allure of selling out is easy to see."[61] Brands that betray themselves should listen to these words of advice sung by pop star Katy Perry: "I stood for nothing so I fell for everything." Too bad more people in companies don't *Roar* like that.

Why do so many brands continue to drift outside of their lanes? Remember, as noted in Chapter 2, *You Don't Own The Brand;* consumers hold the dominion over what a brand means. Companies may also fail to understand that consumers have jurisdiction over brand *latitude*. While Toyota was forced to pay $1.2 billion for covering up safety problems related to "unintended acceleration"—and briefly lost its global sales leadership to GM in 2011[62]—it was back in the driver's seat a year later. This rapid rebound shows a high degree of brand forgiveness from consumers; likely attributed to all the years Toyota filled its brand tank full with reliability equity. In contrast, a similar scandal rocked Audi in the 1980s, but its brand nearly disappeared domestically when sales plummeted from 74,000 units in 1984 to 12,000 units in 1991.[63] This indicated a lower level of brand mercy from consumers—likely because it hadn't yet built a brand reputation around something important to people.

When you steer ideas, products, or services outside your brand's lane—essentially, the perceptive "white lines" that consumers place around your brand to ensures it stays authentic—history shows you will dilute it and people will no longer have a compelling reason to choose your brand instead of a competitor's. Suppose AARP opened its membership to 40-years-olds and USAA offered its products to those with no ties to service? Would AARP still earn $1.44 billion in operating revenue[64] and would USAA's net worth have climbed from $18.7 billion in 2010 to $26.7 billion in 2014?[65] Unlikely, since brands that try to appeal to everyone ultimately appeal to no one. Case in point is Sony, which seems to have its fingers in everything that requires a power outlet including TVs, phones, computers, cameras, and video games. While Sony earned $556 billion in revenue over a 10-year stretch in the mid-90s to mid-2000s, its net margin was a measly

0.9%. In comparison, Nintendo, which only makes video game players, earned just $43 billion during the same period but its net margins were 13 times greater than Sony's.[66] Diversified businesses may win revenue battles but focused brands are more likely to claim victory in margin wars.

USAA, with over six million accounts, and AARP, with its 37 million members, are proof that exclusion can actually be more inclusive than you might realize. Yet exclusion won't work if there are "shades of gray."

What Are Shades of Gray?

Much like what happens to people who struggle to see where they end and other people begin, brands with poor boundaries are vulnerable to losing their own identity. "Shades of gray" are things that companies and organizations do or overlook that muddy their image. For example:

-A fast food chain added premium items to its menu but the process needed to provide those items slowed down their operations.

-A medical research institute with a mission rooted in preserving life formed philanthropic partnerships with fast food and alcoholic beverage companies—both offering products that can contribute to diseases.

-An education non-profit for marginalized students trying to distance itself from the image of being "elitist" agreed to let an Ivy League school publish a white paper about the organization.

While those are isolated examples that might seem benign on the surface, shades of gray often metastasize inside organizations and inflict brand damage by "a thousand cuts." This is particularly true when a company doesn't have a brand mission and doesn't hold people accountable to it. What would Dyson be if it brought ordinary products to market? What if Ritz-Carlton treated people like ordinary Joes?

Without putting guardrails in place, it's easy for brands to stray outside the perceptive white lines established by consumers. Doing so can result in mistakes such as Hooters Airline, Zippo perfume, and Dr. Pepper Marinade. When it happens, consumers *and* employees become confused, and companies can lose millions of dollars, brand equity, and their best employees.

Gray is BADD

Why do companies create shades of gray with their brands? Often, it's because they suffer from Brand Attention Deficit Disorder (BADD). The most common symptoms of BADD are the inability to remain focused on—or true to—the brand.

BADD rears its ugly head most frequently when businesses attempt to attract more consumers. The irony is they eventually chase away the very customers who helped build the brand in the first place. Radio Shack was once a go-to source for electronic and computer accessories as well as select house brand products. It rode that horse for 15 years of steady growth, peaking at $6 billion in annual sales in 1995. Over time, though, it added non-house brand items such as TVs, cameras, and cell phones—products consumers could get elsewhere. Annual sales and stock prices steadily plummeted to the point that "The Shack" collapsed and filed for Chapter 11 in February 2015.[67]

Brands that avoid shades of gray do so by abiding by two important ideals: 1) Conviction for what makes their brand special and 2) courage to avoid anything that could conspire against it. Fishnet Security *only* does IT security and in 2012 secured half a billion in revenue.[68] Intel's adherence to making components for "inside" devices yielded over $50 billion in 2013 revenue.[69] Pixar's lone focus on animated family movies was good enough for Disney to shell out $7.4 billion to acquire it in 2006.[70]

Provided USAA, AARP, Fishnet, Intel, and Pixar maintain brand fidelity and quality, each should be able to sustain their success. Short of an apocalypse coming, there will always be military and public safety service, people living to 50 and beyond, security threats to company data, consumer demand for better technology, and procreation that will ensure future generations of animation movie lovers. All those examples have reached a brand parallax: Singular position, broad impact.

Ries's Law of Expansion

When companies step beyond consumers' perceptive limits, legendary branding guru Al Ries explained that they violate his Law of Expansion. "The power of your brand is inversely proportional to its scope," Ries said. "When you put your brand name on several products, indeed, the line extension allows an increase in sales in the short term, but it undermines the brand name in the mind of the consumer in the long term."[71] Ries added that not only do you lose credibility; you also open the door for a more focused competitor to steal your market share. I liken it to a con artist who assumes more than one identity. Eventually, he'll be exposed and then the jig is up.

Enemies of Brand Boundaries

Without brand boundaries—the guardrails *you* put in place to protect the fidelity of your brand (like Google banning display ads to preserve its "search" image or Mulready's embargo on paper cups to conserve it's beer enthusiast reputation)—gray will find a way in and contaminate your brand. Two of the most common violators of brand boundaries are partnerships and innovation.

Partnerships typically require compromises, which the very best brands avoid. In 1999, Chrysler and Daimler-Benz decided to merge. It wasn't cheap either, costing the companies an estimated $36 billion combined to do the deal. It got even more expensive when eight years later they divorced and Daimler was out billions more.[72] During their rocky relationship, global sales of Mercedes Car Group lost ground to Japanese brands. A year after the split, Daimler CEO Dieter Zetsche admitted it was a bad marriage from the start. As he said, "The reality was that we couldn't actually achieve global integration because it was at odds with the image of our brands, the preferences of our customers, and many other success factors—all of which were far more diverse and fragmented."[73]

Everywhere you turn today, it seems company leaders are on the *innovation* and *disruption* bandwagons and encourage their teams to "think outside the box." But without brand boundaries, you can easily end up with costly extensions like Arizona (tea brand) Nachos 'n' Cheese Dip, Samsonite coats, and Paula Deen kids furniture. Or, potentially worse, nearly bankrupt your entire company like LEGO.

David Robertson, author of the book, *Brick by Brick: How LEGO Rewrote the Rules of Innovation and Conquered the Global Toy Industry*, details in a 2013 *Time Magazine* interview how LEGO's declines in the 1990s and 2000s can be attributed to "out of the box thinking (that) almost put them out of business."[74] Some of LEGO's innovations included snap-together action figures, virtual versions of its product, and even a television show. "There were a couple of really big hits, and in a way, those were really dangerous for Lego because [they created] a thick layer of cosmetics that hid a pretty ugly business underneath," said Robertson. Ultimately, "Lego kind of got away from what it knew how to do," he added.

How did LEGO reconnect with customers and turn its brand around? "They went back to the brick, and they focused more on the police stations and the fire trucks and the other things that not only were what their fans wanted, but were also pretty profitable for them," said Robertson.

Perhaps the message from CEOs to team members should be "Let's think *inside our* box." It worked for LEGO. "When they went back in the box, they found that there was a lot of money in the box and that fans returned to the brand," said Robertson.

Teresa Carey of Performance Pointe, which provides leadership development and organizational strategy to Fortune 500 companies in Pre-Rapid Growth stage, challenges her clients to innovate within the framework of their brands. "Entrepreneurial thinking is doing the same thing but in a different way," she said. "You take an existing process, product or service and even the slightest adjustment can make it more innovative."

Trailblazing within your brand's boundaries should be promoted and rewarded. For example, the essence of the Volvo automotive brand (and likely its perceptive limit) is safety. The first to use laminated glass, three-point seat belts, and side airbags, the Swedish automaker thinks like an "*intra*preneur" instead of an entrepreneur. A recent shift to personal safety has yielded technologies that can detect the heartbeat of someone hiding inside one of its vehicles, alert drivers to drowsiness, and spy potential trouble with vehicles a few cars ahead. In 2014, Volvo reported it set a global sales record.[75]

When it comes to partnerships and innovation, the question to ask yourself more than "can we do it?" is "*should* we do it?" If it's going to shade your brand in any way that doesn't allow it to be "true blue," you shouldn't hit the brakes. Quite often I remind clients what they *don't* do can have a greater impact on their brand's success than what they actually do.

Cultural Impact of Poor Brand Boundaries

Amongst the most egregious violations against brand boundaries is the introduction of ideas, products, and services outside consumers' perceptive tolerances for your brand. Expansion in such ways can sabotage your brand's value and profitability; it can also disaffect the very people you need to execute it.

A 2013 *Forbes* article titled "Six Reasons Your Best Employees Quit You" referenced a Gallup study on employee engagement. It showed "a direct correlation between employee retention, customer metrics, productivity, and profitability when employees see that the mission or purpose of the company makes them feel their job is important." [76] Thus, a company whose purpose is unclear or a moving target can create a climate of chaos. Once your brand starts to fray *internally*, it inevitably unravels *externally*.

In the past few years, Kansas City-based Boulevard Brewing Company began brewing up more than just craft beer. I admit a weakness for their Tank 7 and seasonal Ginger Lemon Radler and would have no problem sporting one of their caps or shirts to show my affinity. But offering Boulevard Pale Ale Mustard and Boulevard Beer Soap? That's where I draw the line, and I suspect their loyal consumers will too—eventually. Whether Boulevard's mustard and soap are good or bad products isn't the point. The decision makers have run afoul of what Boulevard represents in consumers' minds and potentially weaken the brand. Would you drink Grey Poupon Porter or an Irish Spring IPA?

More important is the question of its impact on employees who might be thinking, "I thought I signed up to make specialty beer? Am I working for Boulevard or French's?" Company founders should be asking themselves why they started the company—because of a passion for craft beer or condiments? Its unlikely customers were knocking down Boulevard's door begging it to make soap or lining up for mustard tours.

This brings us to what I say is the most dangerous word in brand: It's those last three letters—the "and" in brand. Brand has always been singular and a synonym of focus and an antonym of vague. You can't specialize if your brand claims to do this AND that. In consumers' heads, Netflix doesn't do streaming *and* downloads and DeBeers isn't diamonds *and* pearls. Thus Boulevard Brewing shouldn't be beer *and* condiments *and* soap.

And *your* brand should never include an "and."

Expand Beyond Boundaries; Contract Your Brand's Value

When you expand your brand beyond its boundaries, you eventually contract its value. It's like a handyman who will paint, do small repairs, cut your grass, clean your gutters, and almost anything else you need done around the house. He thinks being a jack-of-all-trades provides the convenience of a one-stop shop. But as a consumer, I wonder what he does best? I also think he just wants in my wallet. Typically, a handyman—a generalist—will charge less than say a plumber or electrician—both specialists. But like any brand that's a master of none, low price is often the only advantage they have. Remember, most people won't pay a premium for ordinary.

Ultimately, your brand is a covenant with your consumers. When you promise something such as 100% of every dollar donated goes to research, consumers expect every penny will go there. In their minds, a promise is a promise—and a broken one can lead them to lose confidence in your brand. Which do you trust more for GPS: Garmin or Timex? For a luxury car: Lexus or Kia? For jackets: North Face or Samonsite?

Consistency Begets Traction

Like any relationship, you'll get more traction through consistency. So, when businesses color outside the perceptive lines consumers have assigned to the brand, they undermine that congruency and the very thing that attracted people to it in the first place. Millard Drexler, Chairman of the Board and CEO of J. Crew, gets it. He said, "People like consistency. Whether it's a store or a restaurant, they want to come in and see what you're famous for."

Making conservancy, *not* expansion the priority for your brand is difficult because company leaders are constantly under pressure to grow the business. But, as referenced at the beginning of this chapter, Al & Laura Ries of Ries & Ries Consulting say that nine in 10 brand extensions fail. If you only have a 10% chance of success when attempting to expand the brand, then the converse must be true—a 90% chance of success when you focus on protecting it. Remember, you can always take your new ideas and channel them into new brands. When Gap Inc. decided to launch a women's active wear brand, it created Athleta (not GAPleta)—just like it had done previously with Old Navy for stylish and cost-conscious consumers. A multi-brand strategy can be the ultimate in brand protection.

Staying in your brand lane isn't being cautious. It's being bold. Peggy Noonan, author of books on politics, religion, and culture and columnist for *The Wall Street Journal*, captured the spirit of this notion perfectly: "Part of courage is simple consistency."

8 YOU'RE ONLY AS GOOD AS YOUR WORDS

Working for a small agency early in my career had many advantages like being able to dabble in different areas of the practice to see where I best fit. Though, I eventually gravitated toward the strategic side, I've always had creative cravings. In the late 1990s while at the eight-person business-to-business boutique Jewell-Baker-Zander, I got plenty of chances to satisfy them.

One of the agency partners, Martin Zander, was a curmudgeonly, pipe smoking, typewriter-wielding copywriter with decades of big agency experience. He never seemed concerned when other agency partners would also ask me to submit copy to clients for consideration. I loved copywriting and thought mine was generally on par with his if not occasionally better. Yet, without fail, clients always chose his version. Baffled, I approached him one day and asked why. "You see," Martin said between puffs, "there can be a lot good options—even good ones like yours. But there's only one *right* choice."

Sticks and Stones…

Would you prefer a Chinese gooseberry or a Kiwi? Backrub or Google? *Love Song* or *The Sound of Music*? For the record, a Chinese gooseberry is a Kiwi, Backrub was the original name for Google, and *Love Song* was the first name for *The Sound of Music*. What if those brands had gone with their initial iterations—would those word choices have been as effective?

What can be harmful is a brand name that has been tainted by bad publicity, disaster, or scandal. Arthur Andersen's link to Enron prompted its name change to Accenture. ValuJet's 1996 crash in the Florida Everglades that killed all 110 onboard resulted in its rebrand as AirTran.[77] Then there's professional soccer team Sporting Kansas City that dropped LIVESTRONG from its stadium name after Lance Armstrong was exposed as a cheater.

As noted in Chapter 4, *Stop Thinking Like a Business*, another compelling reason to rename is when it's no longer in your control. A good example is the legendary barbeque joint, Oklahoma Joe's, which changed the name of the Kansas City locations to Joe's Kansas City after business partners split and divided up the properties.

If your name gets confused with another, you might consider an alternative. One of the more befuddling to me is *Kansas City*. When I tell people I live there, the first question I get is "Kansas or Missouri?" It's no wonder since Kansas City Kansas—known in these parts as KCK—and Kansas City Missouri—referred to as KCMO—are actually two different cities in different counties with separate governments. Not only is the name the same, there's virtually no geographic separation outside of state lines and road signs. Kansas City is, in effect, riding two horses with one ass.

If given the opportunity to work on the KCK brand, I would strongly encourage it to change its name. KCK has always been seen as the redheaded stepchild to KCMO, which has enjoyed a renaissance the past decade. In 2014, *The Huffington Post* named the Missouri version "THE place to be" because "the food is amazing, nearly everything is affordable and the people are nice."[78] The city boasts premiere downtown venues such as Sprint Center and Kauffman Center for Performing Arts. The addition of light rail to connect its eclectic arts, shopping, and music districts and a four-fold increase in population the last decade[79] have contributed to KCMO's turnaround. Consequently, it has further driven a perceptive wedge between the two cities.

Some people in KCK might argue for riding the coattails of its eastern brethren. I *always* argue against putting the fate of your brand in someone else's hands. Simply put, you can't control what the other one does. After all, it was only a decade ago that downtown KCMO was more bust than bustle. While it seems to be pushing all the right buttons now, it could be a change in city leadership or departure of a couple major employers away from reverting back to the Rumpelstiltskin it once was. If KCK did change its name, I'm guessing it wouldn't get any pushback from KCMO. After all, how many of us really like it when little brother tries to take credit for what big brother does.

One Word Can Change Everything

Changing your brand name is a strategic decision and one that shouldn't be made in a subjective vacuum. Sometime around 2006, an energy company was trying to convince landowners in Dallas County, Iowa, to sell so they could build a wind turbine power plant. At the time, the energy company believed certain natural geological formations there created the optimum environment for storing wind-generated energy underground.

Leaders with Iowa Stored Energy Plant (ISEP) knew it would be an uphill battle in persuading landowners to sell. Those same leaders also weren't making it easy on themselves or Julie Kraft, senior consultant with Frank N. Magid Associates—the firm they hired to conduct research and develop a plan to win landowners over. However, there was a big mountain, er, hill (it's Iowa after all), in the way. ISEP leaders had a strong attachment to the name, Iowa Stored Energy Plant. Kraft, lead strategist on the project, recognized it would be a barrier to success and knew something needed to be done about it no matter how dug in ISEP leaders were. "Who would want to live near a *plant*?" Kraft rationalized to them. She was right. The first battle wasn't at the negotiating table. Rather, it was negotiating the minds of ISEP leaders.

While I wasn't assigned to the project, Kraft asked me to weigh in since she and I had history when it came to positioning clients. Once, we developed a successful brand and strategy for a client over beers at a bar. During our ISEP brainstorming, it occurred to me that they could keep their beloved acronym and still change public perception in their favor. Rather than calling it a "plant" I suggested they call it a "park."

"Who wouldn't want to live near a 'park'?" Kraft later proffered to ISEP leaders. Not only did they embrace the new iteration, it inspired them to come up with a new park-like design. The new name, appearance, and deft public relations strategy engineered by Kraft ultimately changed the landowners' minds.

Sometimes, one little word can change everything. "You have to be mindful of those connotations people have about words, messages, and perceptions," said Kraft. "Word choices are critical. You can't take them lightly; you should be very careful and deliberate, and you should not rush. Take your time to get it absolutely right. If it's wrong, it's going hurt you in the long run."

While the simple but powerful change in positioning turned the tables in ISEPs favor, what truly drove their success was making consumers the king of the hill—the focus of Chapter 2, *You Don't Own the Brand*, and a central theme that runs throughout this book. As Kraft explained, "It's all about the customers and what they want and need. So many times company leaders think it's all about them but it's really about tapping into what their (consumers) perceived needs are."

Brand Conditioning

The first impression your brand creates with consumers can be positive or positively lethal. I wonder if Kodak had built a position around "images" and Blockbuster around "home entertainment" from the start, would consumers have perceptively grandfathered in those brands as their technology preferences changed—like they did with Netflix? By building its image more on depth of content than the delivery mechanism, Netflix seamlessly navigated its transition from snail mail to online.

It's easy to play Monday morning quarterback but the Kodak and Blockbuster examples do teach us an important brand lesson in today's complex, competitive, and ever-changing world. How your brand is positioned *from the outset* can perceptively condition consumers for expansion or shifts. Here's an example.

For the past few years, my firm has worked with a former financial-sector-CEO-turned-entrepreneur who has invented a patented pet tag connector. It makes the traditional metal split ring for pet tags look like a typewriter to a computer. We helped develop the brand name, LINKS-IT, and the positioning very carefully. Being sensitive to the inventor's goals of potentially bringing his brainchild to other categories, we recommended articulating it as LINKS-IT *for Pets* to establish the expectation of future applications, such as LINKS-IT *for Keys* and LINKS-IT *for Luggage*. If it were just LINKS-IT Pet ID, the risk would be greater of creating a connection to pets so stitched into consumers' heads that they couldn't undo it—like Kodak and film and Blockbuster and video.

Create Brand Bridges

In certain situations including partnerships or repurposing, a simple thing I call a brand bridge can be a lifeline. A brand bridge is a word or phrase that creates a cognitive connection between brands while simultaneously preserving their separate identities. A brand bridge can mitigate confusion and condition the mind for future applications. For example, the operative in the LINKS-IT positioning is "for"—and it's a three-letter brand bridge that could allow LINKS-IT to thrive in multiple categories.

For two media brands, a two-letter brand bridge delivered emancipation. Here's how. Shortly after the Disney Company purchased the sports TV network ESPN in the 1990s, it began integrating sports programming with its ABC network property by sharing broadcast platforms, talent, graphics, and more. However, viewers weren't sure if they were watching ABC or ESPN—and that uncertainty threatened ratings. Once again, a simple but powerfully effective brand bridge did the trick. By inserting "on" between networks—ESPN *on* ABC—it helped clarify which network they were watching and where.

In another example, Van Andel Institute (VAI) is a biomedical research institute in Grand Rapids, Michigan, started by a co-founder of Amway. The non-profit has a marketing and fundraising arm called Purple Community. While VAI and Purple Community work for the same cause, they serve different audiences. It's much like the way sibling brands Old Navy, Gap, and Banana Republic target different customer segments.

However, unlike the Gap Inc. family of brands, VAI and Purple Community need to show their connection without creating confusion. I recommended they always refer to Purple Community as an "event." As an example, they'd say, "A Purple Community *Event* to benefit Van Andel Institute." The word "event" becomes a brand bridge that simultaneously connects but separates the brands.

On occasion, it is actually necessary to eliminate a brand bridge to provide clarity. Early on, consumers were confused about the focus of Van Till Family Farm Winery. The study we conducted for them in 2011 showed that 29% of people saw them as a restaurant and 11% as a winery—despite having "winery" in their name. It didn't help that they were going by the name "Van Till Family Farm & Winery." The ampersand was implying that it was about more than one thing. In addition to re-engineering the entire brand position, we convinced the client to eliminate the ampersand and go with "Van Till Family Farm Winery" to convey their winery only intentions. The 2015 research we conducted showed progress with nearly 53% of people now seeing it as a winery.

In the right situations, offering your brand as an additive or extra element can provide leeway for expansion while protecting its integrity. In Chapter 7, *Stay In Your Lane*, I noted how Boulevard Brewing Company took a bite out of the brand extension apple by introducing mustard and bath soap under the Boulevard banner. But suppose it had taken more of an "Intel inside" approach and licensed its Pale Ale to an existing mustard brand as a featured ingredient? "Ba-Tampte mustard *infused* with Boulevard Pale Ale" is a lot easier to perceptively swallow than "Boulevard Pale Ale Mustard."

Connecting by Further Separating

The notion of "connecting by further separating" can be quite beneficial for brands that share a common feature or attribute. If you think Kansas is just flat, flyover country, you've likely never been to the Flint Hills that rise majestically over 82,000 square miles of South Central Kansas. While presenting to the Kansas Flint Hills Tourism Coalition—an organization designed to unify manpower, brainpower, and resources to attract more visitors to the area—I suggested they needed 22 brands, not one. My reasoning? The Flint Hills courses through 22 counties. If each one claimed the same image then tourists would only need to visit *one* county. If you can't ride two horses with one ass, how can you expect to ride 22?

In this case, I postulated that each brand could be rooted in Flint Hills DNA but separated into 22 strands. For example, Chase County's thread would be about "Healing in the Hills" (as in mind, body, and spirit, which was our recommendation when repositioning the county in 2013). Other counties might adopt narratives around Flint Hills art, history, and so on. Through perceptive demarcation, they would benefit their individual counties *and* the entire region by providing 22 unique reasons to visit the Flint Hills—and 22 places to spend money!

The semantics are paramount for any brand that needs to draw a line in the sand—as all brands should do anyway. For example, at the heart of one technology brand we work with is "impartiality." So we counsel the company leaders to avoid using terms like "partners" or "alliances" to avoid any hint of favoritism, and encourage them to use words like "vendors" or "manufacturers" when describing product suppliers. Not only do those terms help protect its non-partisan image, they make it clear to the vendors or manufacturers what their role is in the relationship.

Remember, if your brand doesn't clearly stand for something then it can't stand against anything.

Recast to Reposition

Another type of repositioning is recasting. Recasting is saying the same thing but in a different way to provide more clarity and consumer connection. Around 2005, while consulting a television station in Seattle with Frank N. Magid Associates, a research and strategy firm in entertainment and media, we tested a weather concept distilled two ways to determine which best connected with consumers. "Weather on the 7s," and "You're never more than 7 minutes from your next weather update" were the contenders. The latter won out rather handily with viewers. Such an outcome is likely to be more surprising to marketers who prefer cleverness than to consumers who seek clarity.

In another example, while "Give Us 15 Minutes and We'll Save You 15% or More on Car Insurance" isn't catchy—the main criteria for so many marketers—like "You're in Good Hands With Allstate," it clearly conveys what makes Geico unique and that allowed it to pass Allstate in auto premiums collected in 2013.[80]

A specific message like Geico's is often nixed because of the length. So I find it refreshing that someone at Geico green-lighted the longer but more strategic positioning. When I propose such ideas, clients commonly challenge me by saying, "That won't fit on a business card." My typical response is, "Then you need a bigger business card!" Allowing length to dictate message (with few exceptions such as Twitter whose strategy is predicated on a character quota) is essentially allowing a *tactic* to be in the driver's seat instead of *strategy*.

Go Deep

Another worn-out reason I get for why message or copy should be short is consumers' shrinking attention span. Much like people thought music videos would kill radio and DVRs would be the death knell for television commercials, believing shorter copy is always better is pure poppycock. Ira Kalb, professor of marketing at the Marshall School of Business at USC and president of Kalb and Associates, wrote that it's not about copy length but about the interest to the receiver. "Good marketers know that only members of the target audience can decide what is 'too long' and what is 'too short,' " he said. "If people are really interested in something, they want more. If they are not interested, they want less. You cannot have too much of a good thing, but any amount of a bad thing is too much."[81] Kalb also referenced a series of copy-length tests on website conversions by research laboratory Marketing Experiments. In all of the lab's tests, the long copy outperformed the short copy by "wide margins."

When asked how long a man's legs need to be, six-foot-four-inch Abraham Lincoln quipped, "Long enough to reach the ground." I don't champion longer narrative. Rather, I advocate for depth. Content will always be king—and if it's compelling, then its length is irrelevant. Ultimately, I believe you say only what you need to and nothing more to get your message across. Enough said.

Be Specific

Specificity is often the key to separating and clarifying a brand. For example, you could "start a new program to help teach women basic maintenance" or "start a new program to help women suddenly single by separation, divorce or widowed, learn basic household and car maintenance." Which one of those statements is most likely to find its audience?

However, specificity doesn't mean citing every little detail. Outback Steakhouse's "No Rules" doesn't say it all but it conveys it all to employees when it comes to customer service.

Specificity also means *avoiding claims* such as "best," "unique," "safest," and so on. These are vague and company-centric, not consumer-oriented. They are also *results;* they're not reasons to choose your brand. For example, if I walked into a room full of people and proclaimed, "I keep you safe," would they believe me? Unlikely. Instead, if I focused on reasons such as, "I've got cameras in every room, fingerprint identification at the door, and a security guard twenty-four seven," do I keep you safe? More likely. *Reasons* provide the credentials that will lead consumers to concluding you are the best, most unique, or safest rather than just stating it.

In much the same way we prefer buying a pre-owned car to a used car, despite the fact they're one and the same, brand is the psychology of words. So remember this: While there might be a lot of good words to consider, there will only be "one *right* choice" for your brand.

9 CAMPAIGNS ARE NOT A STRATEGY

Just Say No. I'd Like to Teach the World to Sing. Yo quiero Taco Bell. What do those campaigns from Nancy Reagan, Coca-Cola, and Taco Bell have in common? Despite being hall-of-fame caliber and easy to remember, each *failed* to move the sales needle.

Since Just Say No started in the early 1980s, there have been no correlative declines in substance abuse amongst teenagers. Referencing a large U.S. study conducted by a University of Michigan psychologist, a December 2013 article in *Scientific American* revealed that 40% of high school seniors, 25% of sophomores, and 11% of eighth graders had consumed some alcohol in the past month and almost 3% of 12th graders had used cocaine in the last year. The article said, "In an attempt to reduce these figures, substance abuse prevention programs often educate pupils regarding the perils of drug use, teach students social skills to resist peer pressure to experiment, and help young people feel that saying no is socially acceptable. All the approaches seem sensible on the surface, so policy makers, teachers and parents typically assume they work. Yet it turns out that approaches involving social interaction work better than the ones emphasizing education."[82]

Missing the Brand Mark

I discovered firsthand just how off the mark "Just Say No" actually was in the late 1990s while at a small advertising agency. My pro bono client, the Heart of America United Way, was developing a new substance prevention program targeting "vulnerable teens," not ones already abusing. After weeks of traveling from the inner city to the suburbs conducting focus groups with students in grades 8 to 12, two findings emerged. First, the word "no" meant nothing to them. Second, their "vanity" meant everything to them. So if drugs and alcohol made them physically repulsive to the opposite sex, they would be less inclined to partake. These key learnings informed the campaign, which not only filled up the program pre-launch; it created a six-month backlog.

Coca-Cola's 1971 call for peace might have taught the world to sing and inspired a top 40 version of the song, but it apparently didn't teach people to buy more Coke. During the campaign, Coke's sales remained essentially flat, according to a study of Relative Market Share of Soft Drink Market Brands from 1970-2000.[83] I'm not surprised because Coca-Cola's brand is authenticity—not singing lessons. Conversely, its 2014 "Share a Coke" campaign, which showcased given names on the side of cans, increased domestic sales by 0.4% and reversed 11 straight years of declining sales.[84] I'm not surprised because what could be more authentic than seeing your name on the side of a can.

Pop culture in the late 1990s might have been defined by "Yo quiero Taco Bell." It was hard to find anyone who wasn't talking about the spastic little Chihuahua in the TV commercials but harder to find people at Taco Bell as sales declined 6%.[85] The campaign got axed in 2000 and so did the company president.

I've encountered many campaign creators who justify a failure to move the needle as a byproduct of intentions. Excuses include ones like this: "It was designed to build image not sales." When have those ideas ever been mutually exclusive? It's like someone saying they only buy Playboy for the articles.

Typically, campaigns for Apple products provide proof that you can build image and sales at the same time. For example, from 2004 to 2008, it ran a campaign called "Silhouette" for its iPod. As the name implies, it featured silhouetted people dancing to music in front of colorful backdrops as they listened to their iPods. Later versions featured the famous musicians U2 and Paul McCartney. What didn't change was the continued focus on image not features, benefits, and price. Not surprisingly, iPod sales exploded from around $1.5 billion to $22 billion during a four-year period ending in 2008.[86]

Beware of the Campaign Gravy Train

Having spent a few years at an advertising agency, I know firsthand that campaigns are the gravy train. So it was no surprise when an ad agency hired by a large client of mine for creative execution rationalized that four campaigns, each one designed to address a different aspect of its image, were necessary to build brand familiarity. Open mouth, insert hook. If you can't ride two horses with one ass, then why does any brand need *four* different messages?

For example, the "Please don't squeeze the Charmin" campaign helped the toilet paper brand wipe out the competition for nearly 20 straight years.[87] Nike's commitment to "Just Do It" propelled the brand from $800 million in sales in 1988 to more than $9 billion a decade later.[88] And the medication Proactiv squeezes out over $1B in annual sales by consistently reminding us that even celebrities get zits.[89]

What do those campaigns have in common? They are all one-trick ponies that have ridden a singular message rooted in their brand position all the way to the bank.

However, to just blame campaigns for declining sales would be irresponsible. There are too many other variables including unfocused leadership, ineffective company strategy, changes in competitive landscape, shifts in consumer behavior, emergence of new technologies, and last but certainly not least, a defective brand. Therefore, it's equally capricious to credit campaigns for growth. For example, in 2013 communications giant Verizon spent $400 million less than its competitor AT&T in domestic advertising[90] yet had $11 billion more in revenue.[91]

Thinking campaigns are the answer to your brand problem is like believing that playing the lottery is a retirement strategy. A campaign is, and will always be, a *tactic* of a brand strategy.

Addicted to Campaign Crack

I once heard a quote that reminds me of telecommunications company Sprint. It goes like this: "I never make the same mistake twice. I make it five or six times, just to be sure."

By now, Sprint should be quite sure. Particularly after its 2014 campaign disaster, "Framily"—serial TV ads that featured a weird family, including a talking hamster that played the husband to a real woman. It was nothing short of bizarre, if not all together creepy. It was so bad that Sprint's chairman, Masayoshi Son, flew to the U.S. to demand the company's ad agency be fired.[92] Framily was preceded in death by "Everything You Do on the Sprint Network is Important" and "Say No to Sharing and Say Yes to Sprint." In 2013 and 2014, Sprint's customer churn rate for those on traditional pay plans was nearly twice that of rivals Verizon and AT&T.[93] Employee churn has been equally impressive. Since 2012, some 10,000 people have voluntarily left or involuntarily been shown the door—a significant reduction in Sprint's U.S. workforce.[94]

Sprint's issue isn't campaigns; it's a broken brand. Why did it ever abandon "clarity" as its focus? Its origins can be traced to the 1980s "pin drop" commercials, which could have been more than a campaign. Much like what Volvo has successfully done with safety, clarity could have become a position that endured as consumers' needs changed. The message could have made the transition seamlessly from wired to wireless phone service and applied to fewer dropped calls, unlimited plans, and rate wars when those were the battleground. In late 2014, Sprint found a new agency of record in Deutsch Los Angeles, proving once again it's addicted to campaign crack.

Unconditional Success

Campaign thinking is equivalent to playing a slot machine. You can put a lot of money into it but the odds of hitting the jackpot are usually against you. But a well-engineered and executed brand position is much more likely to hit the mark because it relies more on unique value than chance. And when that promise is "unconditional" it becomes an even better bet. Like QuikTrip discovered.

Tulsa-based QuikTrip, known colloquially as QT, is to convenience stores what Kleenex is to facial tissues. It *is* the category in its markets. Every store is as pristine as a clean room at NASA, and its 15,000 employees are uncanny in delivering fast and friendly service at its 600-plus locations. It has over $11B in annual sales and was ranked 27th on the *Forbes* list of America's largest private companies.[95] In 2013 and 2014, it was the top ranked convenience store in a nationwide poll of 5,000 shoppers.[96]

But it wasn't always so. In the early years, QT was sourcing bargain gas and, by doing so, it was damaging both car engines and its reputation. In response, QT upgraded its fuel and began unconditionally guaranteeing its gas, promising to pay for any repairs if its fuel proved to be the cause of a problem.

While QT ran campaigns to get the word out, it was the promise to unconditionally stand behind its fuel quality that had much greater impact than advertising its new policy. The guarantee was eventually extended to cover everything in its stores, and it ultimately became QT's crusade and brand. The standards necessary to guarantee, "guaranteed" transformed the company's ethos on every level and QT was able to win back consumers' trust. Not only does this illustrate the importance of thinking beyond campaigns; it's a stellar example of evolving from a business to a brand thinker.

Advertising vs. Word of Mouth

Surely you're familiar with Whole Foods, Sriracha, and Rolls-Royce, but when was the last time you heard from them? Successful brands like these demonstrate their difference in all that they do, which can minimize or negate the need to advertise. "The key is to recognize that in terms of brand equity, all that really matters is that the customer develops a positive image," says Kevin Keller, professor of marketing at Dartmouth's Tuck School of Business. "Experience or word of mouth is probably the best way to do that."[97]

Actually, it *is* the best way to do that. Stories based on consumers' experiences with a brand get repeated more than taglines or commercials. For example, when was the last time someone asked, "Have you heard Nordstrom's new slogan?" They're more likely to ask if you heard about the time they refunded a man the entire purchase amount for a set of tires even though they've never sold tires.

Advertising may get your brand noticed, but customer experiences are what can make it legendary. A company that truly exemplifies this is

Zappos. *"Powered by service,"* Zappos is a leading online shoe retailer that doesn't advertise. Then again, with the unbridled admiration it receives from hoards of Zappos zealots, it doesn't have to. Check out a few of the nearly 10,000 testimonials on its website:[98]

> *"You guys are amazing! I placed this order at 8:00 pm on Tuesday night and the merchandise was delivered to my door at about 11:00 am on Wednesday. How did you do that???? With soooo many things in this country being very screwed up, it's nice to do biz with a company that knows how to get it right. Kudos to you all."*

> *"We are frequent and satisfied Zappos customers so much so that we really think Zappos went over the top today by offering to send out a replacement piece of luggage. The Zappos organization consistently tries to solve the problems customers may encounter with efficiency and support. Zappos is a model for other businesses to emulate."*

Advertising is Shouting; Branding is Demonstrating

While sitting in church one Saturday evening, I heard evangelist Dr. Leonard Sweet proclaim: "Preach the gospel at all times but only when you have to use words." Dr. Sweet could very well have been pontificating about branding. His sermon reminded me of a quote I heard some time ago: "Advertising is shouting. Branding is demonstrating. When you fail to demonstrate, all you can do is shout." Amen.

Remember, if your product or service is clearly differentiated, you don't need to scream at people. Even though Krispy Kreme, Costco, and Spanx can afford paid media, they don't advertise. Brand thinkers tend to spend their money on product development and employee and customer experience more than advertising. By doing so, they create stories that their customers willingly share with others.

Too often, branding is confused with labeling, which means affixing your logo, slogan, graphics, etc., to things in an effort to create continuity or extensions. Branding *is* actually doing. No example proves this point better than the ice bucket challenge to benefit ALS that swamped social media in 2014. With millions of videos shared of people electing to get ice water dumped on them for the cause and calling others out to join in, the movement raised north of $100 million for ALS research. That represents 3,500% more than the ALS Association received during the same period the previous year.[99]

Campaign Thinking is Contagious

Campaign thinking isn't only the domain of agencies or marketing departments. I once sat across from a CEO who insisted all the company needed to get out of the cellar was the right campaign. He didn't see the humor—and the point—when I responded, "That's like putting lipstick on a pig." Legendary agency executive, Bill Bernbach, the creative genius behind "Avis is No. 2," Life Cereal's "Mikey," and Volkswagen's "Think Small" made the same point less acerbically when he said, "A great ad campaign will make a bad product fail faster. It will get more people to know it's bad."[100]

Not only was that CEO backing the wrong horse; he was clueless to the fact that his influence had infected his entire organization, creating a culture of like-minded campaign thinkers instead of brand thinkers. As always, horse manure does roll downhill.

For the record, I'm not *anti*-campaign. I am *pro*-brand positioning. Even ad guy Bernbach understood that "if you stand for something, you will always find some people for you and some against you. If you stand for nothing you will find no one is for or against you."

I'll take this a step further. Rather than what your brand stands for, your brand should aspire to be an *is* like Google *is* search, Gatorade *is* sports drink, and YouTube *is* online videos. When you are an *is* you are more likely to be a *need to have* rather than just a *nice to have*. But becoming an *is* requires a brand mission and an unwavering commitment to it.

10 ARE YOU RIDING TWO HORSES WITH ONE ASS?

I wasn't originally planning on penning this chapter. Truthfully, a year after I started writing this book, I was ready to be done. Its not that I haven't enjoyed the writing process. It's been a goal of mine for years, and I do love to share my experiences and insights. Hopefully, you've enjoyed reading it as much as I enjoyed writing it. More important, I hope you've found it beneficial and will think about brand differently than before. Even if you walk away with *one small thing* to do differently, then it's been worth it to me.

For this chapter, you can thank editor Christine Moore. She provided the content analysis and many astute recommendations that molded a bunch of thoughts into this book. She suggested adding "encouragement" as a guide or expert would—words of wisdom on next steps, important actions to take, where this advice might go, and so on.

Why disagree with someone who truly helped me transform this book?

If you're looking for something you can do immediately, I suggest conducting an organizational check-up on the health of your brand. You can do it yourself by performing these simple diagnostics:

- Do a self-exam
- Take an x-ray
- Conduct an MRI

Do a Self-Exam

Make a two-column chart to list all the key decisions you've made in the past year. Title the left column **Business Decisions** and write down all the ones you deliberately made to benefit the business. Title the right column **Brand Decisions** and list all the ones you intentionally made to benefit the customer. If you record more on the left side, you are more of a business thinker, and if you register more on the right side, you are more of a brand thinker. *Your goal is to have twice as many in the right column than in the left.*

Next, take a closer look at the ones you listed under **Business Decisions.** Could they have been approached in a way that would have served the brand first and still had a net positive impact on the business?

For example, if a business decision you made was to "increase our margins by raising all prices across the board by 10%," could you have reframed it (only if it was true, of course) as "Improve the customer experience by re-engineering the store architecture to make access to products easier, improve customer flow, and ensure that help from a knowledgeable employee was never more than an aisle away?" The latter would have created additional value for customers and, consequently, allowed you to justify price increases. The former might have benefitted the bottom line but maybe not your customers—and without them, you won't stay in business very long. That brand decision also turned the business decision into a result instead of a self-serving move.

While this might seem like mere semantics, conditioning your brain's muscle memory to think "brand first, business second," is a huge step toward changing the ethos of your company or organization.

Take an X-ray

To give you a snapshot of the present state of your brand, you should take an x-ray of employees' perceptions of it. This is vital for the many reasons already covered in earlier chapters, but it will also illuminate what your stakeholders are likely telling others about your brand. Also, *don't* neglect the opinions of those with responsibility for your brand outside your organization like partners, affiliates, manufacturing reps, vendors, etc. They are ambassadors for it as well.

In this simple procedure, have them individually—and confidentially—answer this question: *What is our brand?* If you get several answers, multiple but unrelated answers, responses that could also describe a competitor, references to your logo, slogan, campaigns, etc., you've got a diseased brand. Don't worry. It can ultimately be remedied with a brand mission and organization-wide strategy to bring it to life.

Conduct an MRI

You'll need a brand mission for this diagnostic and you'll use it like an MRI machine to scan every limb of your organization—operations, sales, business/finance, employee engagement, and marketing, as well as every system, protocol, and standard. This MRI will help you detect where you have *blind spots* (also referred to as "shades of gray" in Chapter 7, *Stay in Your Lane*) that could conspire against your brand. As the name implies, blind spots are hard to detect and even harder to see the potential damage they can inflict on your brand's fidelity.

You must put *everything* under the microscope to uncover the blind spots. And heed this warning: Elements like these will create a breach in your ability to deliver on your brand promise and that, in turn, will create a breach in the most important thing of all: *Trust in your brand.*

Just like you can't be in two places at one time, you can't be both equally a business *and* brand thinker, have a brand that is about this *and* that, and build operational, financial, and cultural models that conflict with your brand position.

Or, as I prefer to say: **You can't ride two horses with one ass.**

ABOUT THE AUTHOR

Kurt Bartolich started GUTS BRANDING in 2009 to coalesce the three beliefs that have defined how he births, resurrects, and repositions brands: Brands should be engineered objectively not subjectively, built from inside the organization out to the customer to ensure promise and payoff are seamless, and brand *is* business, operational, and cultural strategy.

During a distinguished career that spans a quarter of a century, Kurt has provided brand positioning and guidance to Van Andel Institute, The Canadian Broadcasting Corporation, Monsanto Pharmaceuticals, The Iowa Lottery, Choice Solutions, Formical, SUR-TEC, West Michigan Cancer Center, Carondelet Health, Performance Pointe, Emporia Kansas Chamber of Commerce, three political campaigns, and over 30 television stations in North America, to name a few.

He is also responsible for creating category-defining positions, including Pentadontics for advanced multi-discipline dentistry, Pre-Rapid Growth, a new business growth stage, and the first walk-in Migraine Chiropractic Relief Center, and category-killing names, including APParition, the first wireless body wire for law enforcement, LINKS-IT, an innovative pet tag fastener, and CosMedic Dentistry.

Kurt cut his teeth in media marketing before moving on to the advertising world where he became an agency executive. He eventually landed at Frank N. Magid Associates, the global leader in research and strategy in entertainment and media, where he was a senior consultant and go-to brand positioning guru. He has testified as an expert brand witness and is a frequent lecturer, panelist and presenter, including a recurring role as a brand instructor for Kauffman Foundation's *FastTrack,* a distinguished global entrepreneurship program.

When not brandwashing clients, Kurt loves spending time with his daughter, fiancé, friends, and hosting cul-de-sac parties. He is also a fitness enthusiast who has finished four Half Ironman triathlons and four half marathons. If you cut open a vein, you'll find he bleeds royal blue for the 2015 World Series Champion Kansas City Royals!

Kurt Bartolich

ENDNOTES

1. Poll: "Obamacare" vs. "Affordable Care Act," by CNN Political Unit, cnn.com, September 27, 2013.
2. WHO Gives Virus a Name That's More Scientific and Less Load, by Denise Gregory, nytimes.com, April 30, 2009.
3. Dr. Heimlich is Horrified By The Red Cross' Protocol For Saving Choking Victims, by Dina Spector, businessinsider.com, Feb. 6, 2013
4. Bank is Anything But Typical, by Joyce Smith, *The Kansas City Star*, June 2008.
5. Freedom Bank continues to expand executive team, by James Dornbrook, *Kansas City Business Journal*, June 1, 2015.
6. A Confused Customer Buys Nothing, by Annette Franz Gleneicki, customerthink.com, Jan. 25, 2013.
7. Say Goodbye to the Honda Element, Motorworld by Alex Taylor III, archive.fortune.com, Dec. 10, 2010
8. Samsung Emerges as a Potent Rival to Apple's Cool, by Brian X Chen, nytimes.com, Feb. 10, 2013.
9. The Truth About Lying, by Allison Kornet, psychologytoday.com, published on May 1, 1997–last reviewed on January 3, 2012.
10. Pamela Meyer: How to spot a liar, ted.com, July 2011
11. Final poll shows tight races ahead of the Iowa caucuses, Jan. 30, 2016, cbsnews.com
12. Olive Garden sales hotter than its breadsticks, money.cnn.com, June 23, 2015
13. Item Eight: My Company's Mission or Purpose, *Business Journal*, gallup.com, May 10, 1999.
14. Why Your Company Must Be Mission Driven, by Chris Groscurth, Gallup, *Business Journal*, March 6, 2014.
15. How the Ritz-Carlton Inspired the Apple Store, by Carmine Gallo, contributor, forbes.com, April 10, 2012.
16. What Great Brands Do With Mission Statements: 8 Examples, by Christine B. Whittemore, simplemarketingnow.com, May 1, 2014
17. A Visual Comparison of Google, Yahoo and Bing's Revenue, Profit, Market Share and More, by Marcus Taylor, ventureharbour.com, 2013.
18. Rumspringa: Amish Teens Venture Into Modern Vices, npr.org, June 7, 2006.
19. Companies Only Deliver on Their Brand Promises Half of the Time, by Ed O'Boyle and Amy Adkins, *Business Journal*, gallup.com, May 4, 2015.
20. New pub helps Emporia get its Irish on, by Allen Twitchell, emporiagazette.com, May 20, 2013.
21. Business Jargon Makes People Think You're Lying, Study Says, by Jessica Stillman, MoneyWatch, cbsnews.com, July 1, 2011
22. Restaurant Loyalty Varies By Generation, finds Technomic, technomic.com, July 8, 2014.
23. How to Hire Successfully: Focus on Mission, Values, Talent, by Rebecca O. Bagley, contributor, forbes.com, March 1, 2013.
24. Online interview with Karen Cottengim, founder, True North Career Strategy, Feb. 1, 2015
25. 10 Examples of Companies with Fantastic Cultures, by Sujan Patel, contributor, entrepreneur.com, Aug. 06, 2015.
26. Why Your Company Must Be Mission Driven, by Chris Groscurth, gallup.com, March 6, 2014
27. Recruiting staff for better customer service, by Andrew McMillan, Charteris, marketingdonut.co.uk
28. Want millennials back in the pews? Stop trying to make church "cool," by Rachel Held Evans, *The Washington Post*, April 30, 2015.
29. Want millennials back in the pews? Stop trying to make church "cool," by Rachel Held Evans, *The Washington Post*, April 30, 2015
30. CVS stores to stop selling tobacco, by Elizabeth Landau, CNN, cnn.com, February 5, 2014.
31. CVS Cigarette Ban Will Drive Away $2B in Sales, by Susan Berfield, Bloomberg.com, August 6, 2014.

[32] Airlines: A Transportation or Hospitality Business, jdpower.com, May 13, 2015
[33] The Worst Business Decisions of All Time, wallstreet.com, Oct. 17, 2012.
[34] Why Wal-Mart is Winning in Canada, by Laura Heller, contributor, forbes.com, Jan. 23, 2015.
[35] How Starbucks has conquered Canada, by Michael Babad, theglobeandmail.com, May 27, 2014, updated May 28, 2014.
[36] 5 Reasons Target Failed in Canada, by Hayley Peterson, businessinsider.com, Jan. 15, 2015.
[37] The Dumbest Idea in the World, by contributor Steve Dunning, forbes.com, Nov. 28, 2011.
[38] Financial Times Interview with Francesco Guerrera, March 12, 2009.
[39] Oklahoma Joe's fills $1,400 order for Obama, Air Force One, by Robert A. Cronkleton, kansascity.com, July 30, 2014
[40] Oklahoma Joe's founders cutting final business ties, by Joyce Smith, The Kansas City Star via kansascity.com, Sept. 16, 2014.
[41] MySpace – what went wrong: 'The site was a massive spaghetti-ball mess' by Stuart Dredge, the guardian, March 6, 2015.
[42] Wishing on a fallen Starbucks, by Paul R. LaMonica, CNNMoney.com editor at large, July 30, 2008.
[43] *A Changed Starbucks. A Changed C.E.O.*, by Claire Cain Miller, nytimes.com, March 12, 2011.
[44] Millionaire Far From Its Final Answer, by Bill Carter, nytimes.com, August 6, 2009.
[45] Coors Banquet, the original brand, grows while others decline, by Steve Raabe, *The Denver Post*, December 13, 2013.
[46] How Budweiser Went from "King of Beers" to Court Jester, by Mallory Russell, businessinsider.com, May 7, 2012.
[47] A Whole New Ball Game in Beer, by Peter Sellers, fortune.com, June 9, 2013.
[48] Nine Big Companies That Grew Through the Recession, by Douglas A. McIntyre, 247wallst.com, Aug. 2, 2010
[49] Apple's revenue from 2004 to 2014* (in billion U.S. dollars), statisa.com
[50] Income of Chipotle Mexican Grill from 2006 to 2014 (in million U.S. dollars), statisa.com
[51] *Onward: How Starbucks Fought for Its Life without Losing Its Soul*, by Howard Schultz and Joanne Gordon, Rodale Books, Reprint edition, 2012.
[52] BEHIND THE WHEEL/Mercedes-Benz C230 sports coupe; Luxury Limbo Rock: How Low Can Benz Go? By Michelle Krebs, nytimes.com, Feb.24, 2002.
[53] Mercedes-Benz S-Class Sales Figures, Mercedes-Benz E-Class Sales Figures, goodcarbadcar.net, Jan. 1, 2011
[54] Lexus ES Sales Figures, Lexus GS Sales Figures, goodcarbadcar.net, Jan. 1, 2011
[55] Lexus And GMC Are Top-Ranked Brands For Customer Satisfaction With Dealer Service, autos.jdpower.com, March 14, 2013
[56] Most Dependable Manufacturers, J.D. Power & Associates 2013 Vehicle Dependency Study, cars.com, 2013.
[57] Starbucks Takes a 3-Hour Coffee Break, by Michael M. Grynbaum, nytimes.com, February 27, 2008.
[58] Summer sets on Shandy, Leinenkugel looks for a 'halo' effect, by Tom Rotunno, cnbc.co, Sept. 28, 2013.
[59] The busiest Starbucks in America, Vanessa Ho, seattlepi.com, February 12, 2014.
[60] Ries' Pieces, by Al & Laura Ries, ries.typepad.com, October 2009.
[61] 2015 Jeep Renegade, Jeep's latest brand extension is far from overextended, by Jared Gall, caranddriver.com, January 2015.
[62] Why a Massive Safety Recall Hurt Toyota Than GM, by Karl Brauer, Contributor, forbes.com, July 1, 2014.
[63] In Defense of: The Audi 5000, by Paul Niedermeyer, thetruthaboutcars.com, May 3, 2007.
[64] Summary of 2013 Consolidated Financial Statements, *AARP Annual Report*, aarp.com
[65] 2014 Report to Members, USAA Financial Report for 2014, usaa.com
[66] The Power of Focus, by Jacky Tai, guest columnist and principal consultant at StrategiCom, b2bento.com, Aug. 1, 2011.
[67] Radio Shack Files for Bankruptcy, by Matt Jarzemsky and Drew Fitzgerald, wsj.com, February 5, 2015.
[68] Fishnet Security's new owner makes the world the tech firm's oyster, by Alyson Raletz, Reporter- Kansas City Business Journal, bizjournals.com, January 25, 2013.

[69] Intel Reports Full-Year Revenue of $52.7 Billion, Net Income of $9.6 Billion, posted by Intel PR in Intel Newsroom, newsroom.intel.com, January 16, 2014.
[70] Disney buys Pixar, by Paul R. LaMonica, money.cnn.com, January 25, 2006.
[71] *The 22 Immutable Laws of Branding*, by Al Ries and Laura Ries, Harper Business, 1st Edition, 2002.
[72] Daimler pays to dump Chrysler, by Chris Isidore, CNNMoney.com senior writer, money.cnn.com, May 14, 2007.
[73] Mercedes –Benz Admits to Chrysler Merger Mistake, worldcarfans.com, May 22, 2008
[74] Trouble in Legoland: How Too Much Innovation Almost Destroyed the Toy Company, by Knowledge@Wharton, business.time.com, July 12, 2013
[75] Volvo Cars reports record sales in 2014, Volvo Car Group Global Newsroom, media.volvo.com, January 5, 2015.
[76] Six Reasons Your Best Employees Quit You, by Louis Efron, Contributor, forbes.com, June 24, 2013.
[77] 10 of the biggest company name changes in history, by Ana Swanson, *The Washington Post*, Aug. 10, 2015.
[78] America's Top 5 Cities to Keep on Your Radar, by Carly Ledbetter, huffingtonpost.com, Sept. 26, 2014.
[79] Downtown Kansas City, Mo. residential population on the rise, by Melissa Stern, fox4kc.com, Dec. 8, 2014.
[80] Geico Overtakes Allstate as No.2 Auto Insurer, by Steve Daniels, adage.com, March 3, 2014.
[81] If You Think Short Copy Sells More, Think Again! By Ira Kalb, Assistant Professor of Clinical Marketing, Marshall School of Business, University of Southern California, huffingtonpost.com, March 19, 2015.
[82] Why "Just Say No" Doesn't Work, By Scott O. Lilienfeld and Hal Arkowitz, *Scientific American*, December 19, 2013.
[83] Why there's no Pepsi in Cyberspace, theconversation.com, November 13, 2013.
[84] Those Coke cans with names on them increased sales for the first time in a decade, by Dante D'Orazio, theverge.com, September 28, 2014.
[85] Taco Bell Replaces Chief, Chihuahua as Sales Fall, Greg Hernandez and Greg Johnson, Times Staff Writers, articles.latimes.com, July 19, 2000.
[86] Apple's Decade of Explosive Growth: 2001 to 2010, by Frank Fox, lowendmac.com, January 5, 2011.
[87] Birth of an Icon, news.pg.com, November 12, 2012.
[88] The 10 Greatest Marketing & Advertising Campaigns of All Time, by Lauren Sorenson, blog.hubspot.com, May 8, 2012.
[89] Proactiv's Active Ingredient: Celebrity, by Meghan Casserly, Forbes staff, forbes.com, November 30, 2010.
[90] Advertising spending of selected wireless service providers in the United States in 2013, statista.com
[91] Wireless revenue generated by major U.S. telecommunication providers from 2008 to 2013 (in billion U.S. dollars), statista.com.
[92] Ad Review: Sprint 'Framily" is Frankly Frightful, by Ken Wheaton, adage.com, April 07, 2014.
[93] Average monthly churn rate for wireless carriers in the United States from 1st quarter 2013 to 4th quarter 2014, statista.com
[94] Sprint announces hundreds more local layoffs, by Bobby Burch, Reporter-Kansas City Business Journal, bizjournals.com, November 25, 2014.
[95] America's Best Employers, Forbes, forbes.com, October 2014.
[96] QuikTrip, Wawa Are Consumers' Favorite Convenience Stores, Market Force Study Finds, press release, marketforce.com, September 16, 2014.
[97] Some Brands Thrive Without Advertising, by Catherine Valenti, abcnews.go.com, August 23, 2014
[98] Testimonials, zappos.com
[99] The ALS Ice Bucket Challenge Has Raised $100 Million–And Counting, by Dan Diamond, contributor, forbes.com, August 29, 2014
[100] Legends in Advertising: Bill Bernbach, The Original Don Draper, by Zachary Petit, printmag.com, March 12, 2014.

Made in the USA
San Bernardino, CA
21 February 2016